Emergency Salvage™

Life and Death in the OR

by LSC M.D.

DORRANCE
PUBLISHING CO
EST. 1920
PITTSBURGH, PENNSYLVANIA 15238

Dorrance Publishing Co
585 Alpha Drive
Pittsburgh, PA 15238
Visit our website at *www.dorrancebookstore.com*

ISBN: 978-1-4809-5254-6
eISBN: 978-1-4809-5276-8

This book is dedicated to my parents,

Joseph Edgar Cook

and

Virginia Evelyn Smith

Contents

Introduction

This book is written form the prospective of a Thoracic Surgeon who performs Open Heart Surgery in the Emergency Salvage patient. This book is a superficial introduction to our lives. Included are honest statements about the practice and business of medicine. The book is fiction, to keep the lawyers away. But in all fiction is truth. This book is a work of imagination drawn from real-life experiences. If you live in a politically correct world this book is not for you.

Treating dying patients is like war, absolute chaos. The first victim is the truth. Each observer of the chaos has a different truth.

Emergency Salvage™ refers to a situation in which a patient i.e. sick person is actively dying and a surgeon is performing emergency surgery (now) to salvage the patient from certain death. The patient is dying due to a cardiac (heart) or vascular (blood vessel) catastrophe. Generally a critical blood vessel has closed or torn. This option is available in hospitals that perform Open Heart Surgery and a Cardiac or Thoracic Surgeon is available. We are on call 24 hours a day. Other surgeons, General or Trauma Surgeons, are in a similar situation with patients who are bleeding to death.

I am one of the surgeons who performs emergency cardiac surgery in dying patients in the emergency room (ER), the cardiac catheterization lab (Cath Lab), the intensive care unit (ICU) and operating room (OR). The purpose of this book is to offer some insight into the daily medical and logistic problems confronts by a cardiac (chest) surgeon. I am attempting to write this for the lay public i.e. you. Sometimes our hard work to salvage a dying patient pays off i.e. they survive or all the medical resources fail and death takes over.

It turns out that one best chance for survival in the field. i.e. outside the hospitals, is to have your cardiac event, i.e. fast heart rhythm, in a casino. The people and the defibrillator, i.e. shocker, are immediately available. The electricity converts your fast heart rhythm to a normal rhythm.

Life as we know it as a human ends and every individual s end of life is different. Metastatic Cancer (the cancer spreads to other organs) is the slow death. Treatment is marked by all the Major Therapies i.e. surgery, radiation and chemotherapy. You can see the end coming very slowly day by day. You eventually meet you palliative care Physician and hospice nurse for end-of-life care. Their job is to make life comfortable as you progress to your end as a human.

I deal with a different death i.e. cardiac or heart death. Your heart acutely fails in minutes to hours and the rest of your body fails. I have dealt with the quick cardiac death for over 30 years. This is my story about the medical problems of the heart and patients who are near death.

Patients with cardiac problems are quite different than cancer patients. In many instances they need an emergency salvage operation and mechanical cardiac support with machines to support the heart and lungs until they recover from their near-death experience.

What about your Primary Care Physician, if you are lucky enough to have one? In the large corporation like the Cash Clinic they never know you are in the hospital and never see you in the hospital. Remember their job is to keep you out of the hospital.

Historically in the high-risk patients that I have operated on, I have an end of life discussion with the patient and family. I stop for nothing, if you get pneumonia you are on a ventilator until you recover, if you develop kidney failure you get dialysis until you recover, the only thing I stop for is an irreversible stroke that you cannot recover from. If that happens I will withdraw care. My obligation is to get the patient out of the hospital alive and well.

Emergency Salvage™

I called the OR to tell them about the patient, who is actively dying. The question from them is "How much time do we have?" My response is none...we are on our way from the Cath Lab doing CPR.

The following is the classification for patients requiring operations. This is my classifications.

- Emergency salvage constitutes an immediate danger to life requires immediate operation.
- Emergent, constitutes a pending threat to life, limb or organ requiring surgical intervention in one to three hours.
- Urgent, constitutes all urgent cases requiring surgery within 3 to 6 hours.
- Semi-urgent, all patients requiring surgery within 24 hours.
- Elective, patients scheduled in the surgeons normal block time at least 24 hours in advance.

It is important to note that some hospitals, such as the VA, only perform elective cases. Most operations on patients are elective. The term case describes the case cart, which has instruments and supplies that is pulled from the central supply to perform the operation on a patient.

Stabbings and Infections

"Early Days of Heart Surgery"

I am a chest surgeon (thoracic) operating on the hearts and lungs. Before the development of the Heart-Lung Machine in 1953 all we could do was perform operations on chest trauma (knife wounds to lung and heart) and chest infections (puss in the chest) due to TB or bacterial infections. We still perform operations for trauma and infections involving the chest. In the early days, 70 years ago, these operations were performed by General Surgeons, I had to do a General Surgery residency (5-7 years duration) before I could do a thoracic residency. In the First World War, 1914-18, general anesthesia was available to allow operations inside the chest. Many soldiers received chest trauma due to gunshot wounds and bayonets. The results were chest infections. Antibiotics such as penicillin were not available until World War II, 1941-45. Thus, some General Surgeons became interested in lung infection surgery i.e. Drainage of puss. But Heart Surgery (Cardiac) was not possible other that suturing the heart for stab wounds. In order to operate on the inside of the heart it is necessary to stop the heart from beating and stop the ventilation of the lungs. The first successful attempt to develop a Heart-Lung Machine was by Dr. Gibbon in 1953. This was done with the assistance of IBM engineers. New Medical Treatments generally develop from Physicians working with high tech companies include multiple engineers and scientists. Innovation is difficult to do; it took Dr. Gibbon 23 years to accomplish his vision.

Before the Heart-Lung Machine was developed Dr. Lillehei used a parent as the pump to provide blood flow to the child for repair of heart birth defects (congenital heart defects). The parent's heart and lungs kept the child alive while the heart and lungs were stopped. This was the first successful approach to repair holes in the inner heart. One of the criticisms was that the surgeon could kill two patients with one operation. That never occurred but once the Heart-Lung Machine was developed this approach faded away. This technology advance results in machines improving human life. Next pacemakers were developed to treat heart block that could develop in children having correction of birth heart problems. Next came machines for kidney failure, dialysis machines. All of this innovation predates the Federal Drug Administration (FDA). Next a surgeon performed the first cardiac cauterization on himself and routine injection of dye into the heart arteries, coronary angiograms, became a daily occurrence.

Circumstances of Your Death

Many patients with an acute coronary occlusion (occluded heart artery causing heart muscle death) die in the field, outside of the hospital. The Emergency Medical Technicians (EMT) do closed cardiopulmonary resuscitation (CPR) for 30 minutes and the patient is pronounced dead. CPR saves 92,000 people per year, of course your chances of survival are better if your cardiac arrest occurs around people who can do CPR and have a cardiac defibrillator (a shocker).

If your cardiac arrest occurs in the hospital you have a better chance of survival depending upon your problem. If your problem is an occluded heart artery (coronary artery) your best chance for survival is to the cardiac Cath Lab for angioplasty and stent placement. Additionally, we have devices in the hospital to keep the patient alive i.e. ventilators and Heart-Lung Machines.

But there are many other factors that will determine your survival in this emergency situation. The location of your event, if you live in a large city, more hospitals are available and you have a better chance for survival. If a U.S. Senator arrests in Chicago he or she will get quick care during the day. Had the Senator been fishing in a rural area of Alaska, he would die before transport to a regional hospital. People (patients) in the Upper Peninsula (UP) of Michigan or western South Dakota routinely travel 3-4 hours to a hospital having Open Heart Surgery.

Time of day, during the day, from 7 A.M. to 4 P.M. the Cath lab team and OR team are immediately available and in house. During the night and on weekends they are not in the hospital. They have 30 minutes to get to the hospital and generally it takes 10-15 minutes to set up. Thus the time of day affects your chance for survival.

Availability of trained personnel performing emergency salvage surgery requires expert anesthesia, OR Nurses, OR Technicians and perfusionists to run the Heart-Lung Machine. At the Cash Clinic where I worked for 25 years these personnel were available 365 days a year, 24 hours a day. I have worked at hospitals where a dedicated Heart Team was not available.

Additionally you need a room and a surgeon. I have been in circumstances where no room was available or the surgeon was operating on a critically ill patient. In both circumstances the patient dies.

The Team

Cardiac surgery was one of the first miracles of human medicine. Until the development of the heart lung machine in 1953 it was very difficult to keep the patient alive when the heart was stopped. Remember the heart is a pump it pumps blood to the entire body to keep us alive. To stop the heart, repair it, we must perfuse blood to the body. The first pump was the parent who used their heart to pump blood to the child while it was repaired. Utilizing the Heart-Lung Machine we drain blood from the heart, the right atrium, into a machine that oxygenates the blood and we pump it back into the patient. Thus, we can stop both the heart and lungs. A perfusionist runs the Heart-Lung Machine. A critical position.

An anesthesiologist or nurse anesthetist gives a general anesthesia. The patient goes into an artificial sleep and awakens not knowing what occurred. A miracle of drugs and gases.

To perform the operation we require instruments and supplies. OR technicians provided these essential items to the surgeon. It takes hours to set up the case on the back table. The techs know what we need and are always one step ahead of us.

Circulating registered nurses (RN's) bring a patient into the room, prep the patient and provide sterile supplies. They can either speed up or slow down the operation depending upon their availability. Unfortunately today they spend a lot of their time on the computer entering data into the computer. The computer is more important than the patient.

A Physician's Assistant (PA) or RN first assistant acts as the surgical assistant. In some cases there are two surgeons. If the operation is coronary artery bypass, (CABG) the assistant will harvest the saphenous vein or radial artery to use for the bypass grafts.

In the first surgical teams all of the team were Physicians. Additionally the first surgeons were musicians, playing in a quartet. They worked as a synchronized team. That same principle applies today.

Today's surgeon is the quarterback of the team. We have unique skill our job is to intellectually and physically direct the team. If a new problem emerges we must recognize it and direct the team in that direction.

For the open heart to be performed in an efficient manner, time efficient, we have 10 people in the OR, two from Anesthesia, two from perfusion, two OR techs, two circulating RN's, one assistant PA or RN and one surgeon. So we need a cardiac surgery team that works together. If that does not occur the patients outcomes can suffer. One of the challenges of cardiac surgery is to surround yourself with excellent OR personnel. Time is very important when the heart is stopped. Every minute counts.

The Gas Passers

The doctors and nurses that administer inhaled gases and drugs to produce anesthesia are called gas passers. They place a mask over your face and administer a gas that puts you into an artificial sleep. The goal of the gases and drugs is to temporary induce the loss of sensation and awareness. It may include relief of pain, muscle relaxation, loss of memory or consciousness.

The medical specialty started out when a dentist dripped ether on the face of a patient to begin surgery and it produced sedation and pain control. Breathing in the ether gas produced a miracle. The gas blocked both pain and consciousness. The surgeons were able to do a complex operation on a difficult patient. The era of modern operations was born.

Today the gas passers include both doctors and nurses. The doctors are anesthesiologists and nurses with additional training are called certified nurse anesthesiologists. The specialty is broken into different types of anesthesia, general and local. Twilight and dental. The induction of anesthesia with drugs and gases occur thousands of times daily across the U.S. for heart surgery general anesthesia is used. The anesthesiologist sits in a chair at the side of the operating room table. We get to listen to them as they pass gas. As we operate we get to listen to them and the OR music. We get to know each other in detail. They work with multiple surgeons and we work with multiple nurses and doctors giving anesthesia. We create each other's reputations, and decide on who would do our families operation and anesthesia.

We believe that we know who is best at their job. Two different models of anesthesia exist in the U.S. The model at the Cash Clinic was one anesthesiologist, doctor, controlled three nurses in three different operating rooms. The doctors became administrators and the nurses did the work. At one time the doctors did fewer cases but now they supervise a larger number of cases. They became smarter but lost their technical ability of intubating patients and placing central lines. The large hospitals and clinic use this model, the doctors are now employed by the hospital so they are no longer in control of their destiny.

The other model is all doctor anesthesia without nurses. One doctor per patient with the anesthesia being provided by the doctor, additionally the doctor is an independent practitioner not employed by the hospital. I met this model out west in Montana. Thirty-five doctors provided anesthesia for two hospitals and the outpatient surgery center. However, only seven or eight doctors did hearts.

Each model has its advantages and disadvantages. The job of the surgeon is to identify the best of the doctors and nurses and utilize their skills. In the Cash Clinic model it is more difficult to select who you want to do the anesthesia. The case is assigned a nurse and doctor. The surgeon has no say about this assignment.

As medicine has gotten more corporate the individual patient, doctors and nurses have loss control over the patient care. Guidelines have been set up by the government and corporations. If you meet the guidelines, the patient's blood sugar level 12 hours after operation, then the care was good and the corporation gets an additional insurance payment.

The patient can shop for healthcare but it is very difficult. The prices are not available even for elective surgery. When you are dying, it's hard to shop around for the best price. The best doctors operate on the most complicated and sickest patient. In many circumstances their results are not as good as the doctor who does clean elective cases. Thus, the concept of quality if quite elusive.

But all corporations advertise great quality. The results of emergence operations are never as good as elective operations.

The Big One

People have joked about having in "the big one" for years. The big one is a large heart attack. The size of a heart attack is dependent of the size of the heart artery, coronary artery that occludes. If it is a small branch vessel, such as a diagonal, little heart muscle is damaged. However, if it is a large artery, the left main, that provides 70 to 80% of the blood flow to the heart, you have a fatal heart attack, i.e. myocardial infarction. Generally this occurs outside the hospital and the patient suffers sudden death. But occasionally it occurs in the cardiac Cath lab following the insertion of a guiding catheter into the left main orifice. Generally, there is a pre-existing blockage in the left main 50-90% and the catheter tears the artery leading to a complete occlusion. Once the left main is blocked, the heart muscle loses 70 to 100% of its blood flow. All of this depends upon flow through their right coronary artery which has a different orifice above the aortic valve. Once occlusion occurs a fatal heart attack begins and there is no blood pressure. CPR is started and dependent upon the time of day the patient is taken for emergency salvage CABG. It takes approximately 30 minutes to move to OR and be placed on the Heart-Lung Machine. The concerns are cardiac death and brain ischemia, a stroke. If CPR is performed well generally the brain is not damaged and the patient will wake up and be able to function. But successful CPR and CABG may lead to cardiac survival but brain death. A win lose circumstance. Emergency cardiac surgery is chaos, because you do not know what team is available. Things change in a heartbeat. The ribs and sternum is fractured with CPR.

Once the sternum is opened, I must perform open CPR, directly squeezing the heart.

Professionals that are not used to open CPR may stick their finger through the heart muscle. You have to use your palm's not fingers for the CPR. I have performed emergency salvage for left main occlusion many times over 30 years. Early in my career most patients died. Today, if extra corporal membrane oxygenation (ECMO) is available after the operation then survival results are better. The only chance for survival is the occlusion occurred during the day when OR personnel are available. It is very difficult to place the patient on the Heart-Lung Machine while performing CPR. It takes an excellent Cath lab and OR team to be able to perform this within 30 minutes of the cardiac arrest in the Cath lab.

If the patient dies it is a surgical death not a Cath lab death. The interventional cardiologist that produced the left main occlusion with their catheter is not held responsible for the death. The moral of the story, left main coronary artery blockages are bad. That natural history of the disease is that a 70% blockage is associated with 50% mortality for one year. Coronary artery bypass is the best option for dealing with this lethal problem.

The Bad from a Heart Attack

We call this cardiogenic shock. The heart muscle is severely damaged and the circulation, blood pressure fails. Then over several hours the body slowly shuts down. All body organs are dependent upon the heart pump to stay alive.

The call came late in the day from Dr. No. His father was in the cardiac Cath lab for evaluation and shortness of breath (SOB) and chest pain that started two days ago. In the ER his chest x-ray showed pulmonary edema (fluid in the lungs) and his cardiac enzymes were elevated. Because of this he went directly to the cardiac Cath lab, so called because catheters are inserted into the heart and coronary arteries. We knew from prior studies that he had coronary artery blockages.

I had evaluated and consulted on Dr. No's dad 4 months before for chest pain. At that time he had a totally blocked LAD (left anterior descending artery) on the front of the heart and a 60% blockage on the circumflex artery (artery on side of heart). The front of the heart still moved (contracted) and I believed that he would benefit from coronary artery bypass (CABG). Dr. No and his dad went to the Mother clinic in Minnesota for a third opinion. He did not see a cardiac surgeon but a cardiologist. The doctor recommended medical therapy only. Keep in mind the Mother clinic had 300 cardiologists and surgeons, many of whom would have recommended CABG. Remember the opinion from a cardiologist depends upon what they have to offer for your problem. General cardiologists treat with cardiac drugs, interventional cardiologists treat with balloon angioplasty and coronary artery stents to try and improve blood flow to the heart muscle.

At that time Mr. No was really not a candidate for coronary artery angioplasty (PTCA). His most important artery was 100% blocked. His best chance for long-term survival was CABG. However, he elected to go with medical therapy only. In his present circumstance all of those thoughts and decisions were water under the bridge. His present heart attack was set up months ago. Medical therapy alone did not work. His new catheterization showed dramatic new changes in his coronary artery blood flow. Now both of his arteries supplying blood to the left ventricle were occluded and he was in cardiac shock with low blood pressure. Additionally, he had a new cardiac murmur over his chest. A stat cardiac echocardiogram revealed a large anterior ventricular septal defect (VSD). A hole in the heart between the two ventricles. His septal muscle that separates the right and left ventricle was dead and gone only a hole remained. He then started having runs of ventricular tachycardia (heart rate greater than 150 bpm) a lethal cardiac rhythm. What to do? Nothing and death, or an attempted salvage operation. Many times there are no available family to decide upon care, Mr. No was now intubated and on a ventilator. However, in this case the son was a Doctor and present in the Cath lab. He wanted an emergency salvage operation. Additionally, the interventional cardiologist wanted something done, he did not want Mr. No to die in the Cath lab, it would be his death. The results would look bad at the mortality and morbidity (M&M) conference. He wanted a VSD repair and a CABG performed. I had not had an operative mortality (death within 30 days of operation) in the past three months, so l was agreeable. However, if I had a patient's death last week, I would have paused. However, what is the patient's risk, without the operation he would be dead in a few minutes, 100% mortality. What is the average survival for 100 patients having VSD repair and a CABG at one month, probably 30 to 35%. But the survival statistics are for a group of patients. Mr. No has a 100% chance of death or 100% chance for survival. Remember my obligation is to the individual patient. After a serious discussion with Dr. No we were off to the OR. I did not bring up the decision not to operate four months ago. We both understood the window of opportunity for low-risk surgery was forever gone.

The cardiac team was still in house and an OR was available. We were on the Heart-Lung Machine within 30 minutes. The anterior and lateral coronary arteries were bypassed and the VSD was repaired with a Dacron patch. But, almost all of the septal muscle was dead and the patch was large. A successful operation but the heart was stopped for 80 minutes. Mr. No would not maintain an adequate blood pressure when the machine was weaned off. After 6 hours of support we stopped the machines and pronounced him dead in the OR. Mr. No was an operative death from the Cash Clinics viewpoint. However, my view is that he died from complications of his heart attack. Dr. No brought up that question why didn't we operate four months ago. The reason was the outside opinion from the Mother clinic that was unnecessary. Remember second or third opinions may not help but rather confuse care. Such is life; we make decisions every day about our health. But we do not know the consequences for days, weeks, months or years. My job as a surgeon is to aid the daily creation of life and postpone death. But as a surgeon you have to be aware that clinic administrators may use your results against you. Only the paranoid survive.

It is important to remember there is a lot of healthcare advertisement. The Mother clinic wants you to come there for your care. If you can drive or fly you are an elective customer, low risk. The Cleveland clinic or Mother Clinic does not want you when you are dying it only makes them look bad. As I tell my patients the best advertisement is a patient who is alive and happy. As a surgeon I get great emotional rewards from the patient who is salvaged to live another day. It is the greatest gift we receive from the practice of medicine.

The Pump

The heart is a pump, a muscle with blood on the inside it squeezes (systole) and the blood comes out of the aortic valve into the large blood vessel aorta. The muscle squeezes and then it relaxes (diastole). The heart relaxes two thirds of that time (diastole). The heart is a pump; it is not the seat of the soul that is the brain that controls consciousness.

There is a hard shell around the heart (Pericardium). If blood or fluid builds up between the Pericardium and the surface of the heart muscle (epicardium), the heart muscle (myocardium) can be compressed and fail.

Like any muscle, the heart muscle must get blood, between beats to refresh itself to beat again. The blood to the heart muscle (myocardium) is provided by pipes (coronary arteries) that are located just above the aortic valve. Blockages can develop in these pipes, and we call this arterial sclerosis, hardening of the arteries. Think of blockages that develop in your water pipes over many years. There are three main pipes providing blood flow to the heart muscle, one on the front (left anterior descending), one on the back (right coronary artery) and one on the side (circumflex). If one of these arteries close off and blood flow is lost to the heart muscle, you have a heart attack i.e. Myocardial infarction. Of course your heart doesn't attack you, the muscle just dies. If the blockage is in a large artery a large amount of muscle dies. If it is in a small branch artery you have a small infarction. You have enough heart muscle to pump out 65-70 % of the blood in the heart, we call this the injection fraction. The amount of blood in the heart ventricle is 100%. As you have large or small heart attacks the amount of muscle available to eject is reduced. When your ejection fraction reaches 30% then you develop congestive heart failure. The heart muscle is inadequate and blood builds up in the lungs. Heart attacks kill thousands of people every day.

Everything that we do in the cardiology and cardiac surgery world is designed to improve blood flow, stents and coronary artery bypass, to the heart muscle. Your heart muscle is your life, lose it and you die. The coronary arteries, pipes, are the determining factor about how long you live. The chambers in the right side of the heart, right atrium and the right ventricle pumps blood into and through the lungs. The two valves on the right side of the heart are generally immune from disease, i.e. tricuspid and pulmonary.

The left side of the heart collects blood from the lungs and pumps it out the aortic valve. Two chambers exist: left atrium and left ventricle. Two valves that open and close with each heartbeat exist around the left ventricle. The mitral valve between the left atrium and left ventricle and the aortic valve between the left ventricle and aorta. If a valve becomes blocked it is stenotic, if the valve leaks it becomes regurgitate. These valves are commonly replaced or repaired.

Blood pressure is generated by the left ventricle the muscle contracts, squeezes, peak blood pressure results systole. The pulse you feel at your wrist. The muscle relaxes, aortic valve closes, and you lose your pulse, this is called diastole. Your heart rate is the number of times your heart beats every minute. The Normal heart rate is 80 beats per minute (bpm). If your heart rate is slow, less 50 bpm, you have Brady cardia. If your heart rate is too slow your brain doesn't get enough blood and you blacked out, syncope. The treatment for a slow heart rate is a pacemaker which stimulates your heart to beat. Slow heart rhythms in the elderly are a common cause of motor vehicle accidents. They pass out and run off the road. Fast heart rates greater 150 BPM, can also cause you to black out, your heart muscle cannot work due to the fast heart rate

The treatment for this is medications or a cardiac defibrillator that shocks your heart back into a normal rhythm.

If your heart beats 80 times a minute, that is 2400 times an hour, 57,600 times a day, 403,200 times a week 1,728,000 per month

20,736,000 times a year. All adults have a heart that has beaten billions of times. The heart is the most amazing, to me, organ in the body. You can live without a viable brain but not without a heart. The number one cause of death in adults is heart related. A great part of my life has been spent trying to increase the number of heart beats in my patients.

The Big Squeeze
(Compression of the Heart)

The pericardium is a fibrous capsule, think of peel of orange, surrounding the heart muscle. There is fluid between the capsule and the surface of the heart. This fluid protects the heart as you exercise. The amount of fluid is normally small 15 - 20 ml. If a large amount of fluid builds up, 200-300 cc, between the capsule and the surface of the heart, i.e. Pericardium, compression of the heart can occur. If the low pressure atrium, pressure -4 to+5 mmHg, is compressed then blood cannot return to the heart. This results in low blood pressure and a high heart rate. When the heart fails the body starts to fail. Excess fluid squeezes the heart, we call this pericardial Tamponade. The excess fluid can be due to bleeding from a heart (think knife wound), Inflammation of the pericardium (viral or bacterial infection), or cancer (metastatic cancer from the lung).

An 85-year-old male presented to the ER with shortness of breath (SOB) nausea and abdominal pain. His heart rate was 120 bpm (high) and blood pressure 80/60 (low). He was in a renal failure with a serum K+ (potassium) of 6.3 (normal 3.5 -4.5). He had been started on Eliquis to decrease his stroke risk from atrial fibrillation (irregular atrial rate 130 -160) unfortunately; this medication caused bleeding in the pericardium which led to compression of the heart muscle. He had an emergency echocardiogram (ultrasound of heart) which revealed a large pericardial effusion with Tamponade (compression of the heart). He was not making clotting factors in the liver. He was developing multi organ failure. The heart failure was producing a kidney and liver failure. Because of his bleeding risk the cardiologist attempted to drain the fluid with a needle. This failed, the needle punctured the heart muscle and that bleeding worsened. Thus, an emergency salvage removal of the Pericardium was attempted.

I went underneath the sternum and removed part of the Pericardium and 600 cc of fluid. We call this a pericardial window. This removed the squeeze on the heart and the heart rate decreased and then blood pressure increased. His organ failure improved. He was on renal dialysis for a week. Gradually he improved and went home in a week. His goal was to go crappie fishing at Kentucky Lake. He continued to fish and be happy. The timing was good for him.

Gunshot Wound
GSW to the Chest

GSW is a gunshot wound. The ER called, a GSW to the chest was being flown in from Nebraska. I called the OR to get a team and OR for an emergency operation. The history, a 59-year-old female presented to an ER in Nebraska with no blood pressure. She was given two liters of fluid, three PRBC (packed red blood cells) and two FFP (fresh frozen plasma). The first call came to me was at 1:20 P.M., the patient arrived at 2:35 P.M. with the HR-110 and the blood pressure of 70/40, cold and clammy skin, but alert. To OR with Epi (epinephrine) Bolus. Intubated with blood pressure of 60/38 BP. CXR (chest x-ray) shows pellet in left chest, entry wound was at right anterior axillary line at the third interspaced. Patient is still alive due to good ER in Nebraska, good flight team and the airplane. Lady was shot at 11:00 and was in the OR at 2:50. She had survived 3 1/2 hours. She was very lucky, shot with pellet gun and saved by high tech medicine. I preformed sternotomy and opened up the Pericardium. Her right Pleura was open, the Pleura is the lining around the lung, and she had two units of PRBC in right chest and one PRBC in the Pericardium. She did not die of cardiac Tamponade because she was able to a bleed into the right chest. I repaired the entry site, 2 mm small hole, in the lateral ascending aorta and exit wound adjacent to the pulmonary artery.

The next day the patient is extubated and the husband is at the bedside. Now I get the story of the GSW, I never ask when the patient presents to the ER, the story only creates distractions for the patient. The husband was shooting at a bird in a bush and the wife walked out from the bush. The husband did CPR and called 911. He both took and then saved her life. The patient had a right rotator cuff surgery two weeks before the incident. The EMT's and sheriff's deputy arrived and the husband told them to be careful with her right shoulder. He was arrested for obstruction of justice and attempted murder. He was in jail during her transport and emergency operation. The sheriff, who he knew, was at the scene with a new female deputy. The husband said the sheriff was showing the cute female deputy about the power of law enforcement. His lawyer is dealing with the sheriff.

I have dealt my entire career with people who think they are in control of things. Generally they work for the government. But an acute life-threatening illness always changes their perspective. I realize that I am not in control, and I try to aid patients in dealing with the system of healthcare and their illness.

Death and Donuts

Patient outcomes have always been important to Physicians, especially surgeons. The cause and effect are obvious in our surgical care. When we perform an operation our goal is for the patient to benefit. If we remove an infected appendix the patient avoids a potentially lethal rupture and possible death. In the past many patients with a ruptured appendix died. Today a death from appendicitis could be marked as malpractice. Unfortunately good results are not always forthcoming some patients have poor outcomes such as bleeding, infection, stroke or death. However, I see these problems daily without a patient having an operation. In my line of work the outcomes may be determined by how and when the patient presents with their problems. In patients with an occluded heart artery and heart attack, we would rather have performed an operation before the damage to the heart. Unfortunately, that is rarely the case.

As medical students in the early 1980s, my first exposure to complications and death was at Saturday morning surgical Morbidity and Mortality conferences. On the weekend only urgent and emergency cases were performed. Therefore, generally Saturday morning from 8 to 10 A.M. was available for teaching conference at Baylor Houston. The residents call the Mortality and Morbidity conference "death and donuts." A surgical resident presented the patient to attending and residents and discussions occurred over coffee and donuts. Sometimes the discussions were quite heated: "You preformed an operation that killed this patient." Egos were commonly deflated. Surgeons do not accept failure in an easy manner; all complications and deaths from the prior week were discussed. The goal is to learn from other people's problems. It is smart to learn from other surgeons' failures. Today there are no Saturday morning conferences no one wants to go to work on the weekend and work hours are limited to 80 per week. Call is twice a week, life is a leisurely.

One joke in my residency was that every other night call is bad because you miss half of the emergency cases.

Surgeons were the first Physicians to develop quality improvement in an attempt to improve medical care, as an attending, resident and medical student I became immediately involved with M&M conferences for over 11 years. When I came to the Cash Clinic in 1990 there were no mortality and morbidity (M&M) conferences. Over many years we developed a monthly M&M for cardiology and cardiac surgery. It took many years before that Physicians would openly talk about patient management issues and their patience complications such as bleeding, stroke and death. But remember if the patients arrests in the cardiac Cath lab during angioplasty and goes to the OR for emergency CABG and dies. The death is counted as a surgical death in spite of the fact that the cardiac arrest was due to the heart catheterization.

Now the politically correct term is quality improvement. Nurses, Physician assistants, and administrators want to attend. In many instances the administrator's salary is tired to perceived quality indicators. However, Physicians rarely speak up at these conferences, no one individual is responsible for the failure. We talk about system improvements the discussion is about the monetary quality indicator, was the blood sugar less than 140 at 0600 A.M. on the first post-operative day.

The group that I represent the Society of Thoracic surgery (STS) started a cardiac surgery in database in 1989, I participated from 1990-2017, all of my cases were entered. When it started it was about improving the quality of cardiac surgery care. That data was collected of four pages. Today it is a research database that encompasses seventeen pages. No one wants to fill it out due to the time requirements. Additionally the results from 100,000 patients over five years may not apply to the one patient you are operating on. Statistical probabilities based on populations are informative for the population as a whole but not directly for individuals. Our challenge as clinicians is to take care of the individual in front of us, guidelines offer thoughtful recommendations and not the final word.

Administrators today want coronary artery bypass morality rates to be 1-2% at 30 days after operation. But the results are dependent upon how many patients that you operate on who are actively dying. Generally one half of the patients who are operated on as they are dying survive. Without an operation 90% die. Thus, your results are dependent upon how ill the patient is and the presence or absence of an emergency operation.

I have a lot of experiences over 5500 open heart operations, but one year in 200 patients I had a 0.5% 30-day mortality rate for CABG, a good year., However, the next year my morality rate was 5%, same hospital and surgeon.

The good news is today that technology is better and the results have improved for CABG. But the patients are older and sicker and the tendency is to avoid dying patients. But we are always trying to improve our patients' outcomes.

The Prison

Over the years I have had many of my patients remark to me, get me out of here, this place is like a prison. Of course they were referring to the hospital that they had been admitted to. Their goal was to get out ASAP.

It was a point well taken. They were awakened for their vital signs i.e. heart rate, blood pressure, respiration rate and temperature during the night and could not sleep. They were injected drugs and stuck for blood draws. Cuffs were placed on the arm for blood pressure and compression socks were placed on the legs for compression. Everyone was a stranger multiple nurses, Physicians, nursing techs, social workers, and respiratory therapists. It's your body but you don't have much say over it. You signed the agreement to that when you were admitted. Multiple x-rays and CAT scans for unknown reasons.

If they came in for unexpected reasons, chest pain, and shortness of breath or gastrointestinal bleed they are scared and believe they may die. An acute illness does away with your feeling of security, you are concerned about dying. They are no longer a customer but rather a patient. What is happening to me? Illness creates vulnerability in people. The hospital is a maze involving the old and the new. Children are being born and people are dying.

In the past you would have a Primary Care Physician and they would have admitted and cared for you in the hospital. You would have had a personal relationship before hospitalization. Not today, you are assigned a hospital Physician. Additionally you may see multiple specialists for further evaluation. That job of the hospital Physician is to make your diagnosis ASAP and get you discharged ASAP.

In the old days, 1990, you would have been in the hospital 4-5 days. Not today where time is money. I have worked in hospitals where the average hospital days are posted 2.7 days and so is the goal 2.3 days. Hospitals and the insurance company want you in and out ASAP. Hospitals are paid on the basis of your problem diagnostic related groups DRG's; there are thousands of billing codes to describe you and your illness.

You are sort of a captive. If its flu season the hospital is paid to provide your flu shot. They want you to have it regardless of your primary problem a heart attack. The hospital does not want you to fall, so you are told to use your call button. You automatically get heparin injections to prevent deep vein thrombosis even if you don't need the shot.

There are many true prisoners in the hospital guarded by the deputies. They want to stay as long as possible, true jail is much worse that the hospital. Of course the police want them out ASAP because the hospital bills come out of their budget. One sick patient can destroy the county budget. Every patient has a different story.

If you have been admitted following elective surgery you know what to expect and have had preoperative teaching. But if you were peeled off the pavement following a motor vehicle accident (MVR) you may wake up in the ICU with a tube in your mouth on a ventilator. Certainly your goal is always to get out of the hospital, alive.

Problems in Patient Care
"Piss Poor Protoplasm"

Piss-poor protoplasm (P3) with little motivation to live. This is the individual patient that we do not want to operate on. When we do major operations, such as open-heart surgery, on our patients we want them to live longer and prosper. However, many patients present too late in their disease process, badly damaged heart, and cannot be helped. When proceeding with open-heart surgery there are two primary factors affecting their survival the physical and the spiritual. Many physical issues affect the healing and recovery from open-heart surgery. Are they obese, diabetic, have renal failure, bad lungs, cancer or prior stroke? How old, are they inactive and immobile? Do they have an infection or on steroids or blood thinners? A combination of these factors produce piss-poor protoplasm and recovery is questionable. From a spiritual viewpoint, does the patient want to live? The question is do you want to continue in this present life form? Some people are ready to pass from this world; and there is nothing here on earth to encourage continued life. I had had the misfortune to operate on these patients. One was an emergency salvage operation in a lady who was dying from a heart attack. The family said to operate, she was a on a ventilator, with a tube in her trachea (windpipe) unable to speak. Modern machine keeping her alive. We operated, CABG, and she lived. But she was very unhappy with me, as she told me later on multiple occasions I wanted to die and I am mad at you for saving me.

It is hard to understand this in a 73-year-old with much to live for, but some people are unhappy with life and want it to end. Therefore, for my patients to do well after open-heart surgery I need for them to be motivated to live. After the event the emergency operation, and the patient is fighting for their life, some families give up and want withdrawal of care. They believe that life is like a TV set on or off. They do not understand their loved one is in the twilight zone somewhere between life and death. They do not understand that they are not suffering and will not remember the event. The brain does not process memory it the twilight zone. The patient is not alive in the normal sense and not dead, both the body and spirit are trying to survive to maintain contact with our world. They may hear but cannot respond. General anesthesia produces a similar situation you are alive but not aware of the world. The anesthetic wears off quickly, minutes and hours. A recovery from a near-death experience takes weeks to months. I have cared for patients who were in the ICU four months. When they returned to see me in clinic there was no memory of the experience. The body and spirit does remarkable things in order to survive. It is a gray line that exists between life and death and we as Physicians cannot predict the outcome.

Doctor Death

Dr. Death was a critical care Physician who worked in the medical intensive care unit (MICU) at the Cash Clinic. The MICU Physicians are not surgeons (rather critical care Physicians) who deal with ventilators, dialysis and infections. They do not directly deal with surgical illness, blunt trauma (MVA) penetrating trauma (stabbings and gun shots) cold legs or abdominal infections. Surgeons deal with these problems. However, the critical care Physicians deal with these patients after the operation. Most large hospitals had a surgical ICU but not the Cash Clinic. Fortunately I got around these problems. I helped to create a cardiovascular intensive care unit in 1991. Thus, I could manage cardiac, vascular and thoracic patients directly without critical care Physicians.

Medicine is a very political. New groups of Physicians use educated requirements to control groups of patients like a MICU patient. The trauma or general surgeons could operate on patients can but they could not directly care for them after the operation. Only the critical care Physicians could care for patients in the MICU. Critical care Physicians are shift Physicians, on call for 12 hours and then a new doctor comes in. Dr. Death would take over the care of a patient, decide that little could be done, contact the family, and tell them little could be done. After all the explained Dr. Death the patient was being kept alive by machines (i.e. ventilator). He would encourage them to withdraw care. Many a surgeon performed an emergency operation on Friday and return on Monday to find their patient was dead (care withdrawn). This was a recurrent problem and all of the surgeons tried to avoid having their patients cared for by Dr. Death. One of our trauma surgeons was forced out so he contacted the state of Illinois. The state sent in one inspector for one day, needless to say the cover-up was in. You could not be truthful in you desired your job. The hospital administration was OK with this arrangement. A death would open up a MICU bed for a new patient. The number of beds was limited, no one wanted to divert patients due to lack of beds. A new patient brought new cash. Eventually, Dr. Death moved on. He wanted to work fewer hours.

The fact that there are Dr. Deaths taking care of patients was an incentive for me to take care of my patients after operations.

The Stroke Scam

It seems like a good idea, the rapid treatment of a stroke. A stroke is generally related to the occlusion of a blood vessel leading to the brain. However, a stroke can be due to a bleed in the brain. The causes are multiple; it can be due to a large occluded vessel providing blood flow to the brain (i.e. carotid or neck artery) or a small clot moving (embolus) from the heart to the brain. A bleed in the brain or due to trauma (club to skull) or rupture of an artery in the brain (aneurysm) all can cause brain damage. Many times we must rule out a bleed before therapy can occur. Think CT (computerized tomography) of brain.

If the stroke is due to a clot the sooner the clot can be busted up (Lysis) the greater the chance of a limiting damage to the brain tissue. If less tissue is damaged (cell death) then by inference an improvement in arm and leg strength, additionally vision and memory changes would be improved.

Large healthcare organizations such as the American College of Cardiology (ACC) or the American Heart Association (AHA) developed core measures (evidence based medicine) designed to reduce death and brain damage (we call this mortality and morbidity). The government tied 2015 hospital payments to these core measures. All of this sounds good and logical, but it is not. When patients have their stroke outside the hospital they were well and then immediately ill. It is easy to observe when one of our loved ones cannot speak or move. If this as an acute ischemic stroke (fast reductions in blood flow to the brain). Then a clot Buster drug (thrombolytic therapy) given them within three hours of symptoms may reduce the destruction of the brain tissue.

The gray area is a perceived stroke while the patient is in the hospital. This is where the Cash Clinic rakes in the money. They, administration, make it possible for any nurse (RN) to call a code stroke without notifying the patients Physician. If a code stroke is initiated at the Cash Clinic a Physician (hospital employee) who doesn't know the patient must come within 30 minutes and do a consult (fee). Then a CT scan is ordered (charge) which may or may not be indicated. The concept is good (and expensive) but the majority of the called strokes are not strokes.

At the Cash Clinic the code stroke was started in 2009 for hospitalized patients. The first patient that I was caring for postoperative day number one following coronary artery bypasses grafting. I saw the patient at 9:00 A.M. He was doing well. I returned to see him at 12:00, the nurse said his CT scan of brain was normal. I asked why a CT scan, the answer he was acting funny. I asked the patient why were you feeling different, the nurse gave me some IV narcotics. The nurse had overdosed the patient. Then next patient was a patient who had CABG done out for a large anterior heart attack. The epinephrine (stimulates heart muscle) was being weaned off. I received a call from Josh, the new ICU nurse, he had called a code stroke and the hospitalist was ordering a CT scan of head for confusion. I asked about the heart rate and blood pressure, both were low, the epinephrine had been stopped and the patient was in cardiac shock. The epinephrine was restarted and the patient improved, no stroke but a charge was generated.

When I complained to the ICU nursing supervisor, Amy banter, I was told we do not have to notify you about code strokes. The nurse can call them without your input. I later found out 70% of the code strokes at the Cash Clinic did not have a stroke and only 7% of the patients were treated for a stroke. Additionally, when a code stroke is called on a patient a stroke swallow screening test is ordered and the patient is made NPO (nothing her mouth) until cleared by speech therapy. This results in an additional test and consult that is automatically ordered by the corporation. More money for the cash.

I have spoken to other cardiac surgeons at academic medical centers, no one could call the code stroke except the surgeon. Actually, patients after open-heart surgery cannot receive clot busting drugs, they could bleed to death. I am not saying that patients after heart surgery do not have strokes, may do. But the treatment options are limited.

You must realize that there are two forces in medicine, the Physicians who practice and the business of medicine. My job is to care for patients. Healthcare administrators are in charge of the business of medicine. The business involves squeezing the last dollar out of the consumer and insurance company. At the Cash Clinic the patient has a number, a cash number. The Cash Clinic employs hundreds of administrators with MBAs (Master of Business Administration). Their job is to maximize the cash flow.

Stent Time

Today, 2018, the initial treatment for coronary artery occlusion is coronary angioplasty and a coronary stent. The stent keeps the artery from collapsing after the blockage is cracked with the balloon on the catheter. If you make it to the hospital with a cardiac catheterization laboratory the goal is to have you in the lab within 90 minutes after you present to the ER. Removal of the occlusion (blockage) improves blood flow to the heart muscle and reduces damage from your heart attack. Modern medicine at work. But many hospitals do not have cardiac Cath labs or open-heart surgery and the stents do not always work. Additionally, nothing lasts forever.

A 59-year-old male presents with his second heart attack in one week. It's late Friday night. On Monday he presented with a lateral heart attack, his circumflex artery was occluded. It was opened with a balloon, breaks the plaque made of calcium, cholesterol and lipids and a stent was inserted to prevent the artery from collapsing. He was placed on Plavix, to prevent the stent from clotting. This worked for 4 days and the artery closed off again. Additionally, he had an 80% blockage in the artery on the front of the heart (LAD) the widow maker. The cardiologist could have referred him for CABG on Monday. However his plan was to return him for another stent, i.e. the business of medicine. This plan was good for the cardiologist but not the patient. He was unable to open the stent. The cardiologist wanted him to go to OR ASAP. What to do in a patient with two heart attacks in one week. I was concerned about his bleeding to death, due to Plavix, after emergency salvage CABG. I had the cardiologist insert an interaortic balloon pump (IABP) to limit the heart attack and placed him on heparin. I operated in 48 hours, when the bleeding risk was reduced. The timing of an operation is very important. When things are going bad the patient is a hot potato, the cardiologist wants to shift the risk to the surgeon. However, this could have been avoided if the cardiologist had referred the patient for CABG after the first heart attack. The role of the stent and keeping the coronary artery open is variable it can last for hours, days, months or years. Each patient's artery is different. It is important to recognize that benefit of coronary artery bypass over multiple stents. Unfortunately, many patients want a quick fix with little downtime. Additionally, many cardiologists do not wish the patient to have a discussion about an option other than stent and the artery. They would lose business.

Hole in the Wall

As a thoracic surgeon I deal with two major specialties cardiology (heart diseases) and pulmonary (lung diseases). These are the two primary organs in the thorax (chest). Additionally, the esophagus runs through the chest.

The primary cardiologist that I deal with is in the interventional cardiologist. They put catheters, balloons, and stents into the heart arteries, coronary arteries. For their interventions they must place an introducer into an artery in the leg (femoral) or arm (radial). The introducer makes a hole in the artery for their catheters. Once it is removed the hole bleeds, these patients are on blood thinners. Generally the hole stops bleeding with pressure on the hole. However over my 30 years of practice I have repaired holes in coronary arteries (in the heart) and holes in the heart muscle due to pacemaker wires. I have repaired the complications of interventional cardiologists, for years.

In reality the interventional and electrophysiologist (EP) cardiologist produce holes in the arteries and the heart. They are "hole in the wall" doctors. I have been repairing these holes for over 30 years. Over time the holes have gotten smaller for cardiac catheterization and larger for catheters for aortic valve implants. They cannot repair their own complications; they are not surgeons, so I get involved in many complications of the interventional cardiologist. It is like many relationships, they love me, but yet they hate to see me, because I repair holes in the artery and heart for them. I call them the "hole in the wall gang." Overall, they do an excellent job. Their complication rates have improved because the catheters are now smaller.

There are times when I cannot repair the hole in the coronary artery. A patient presented to the Cash Clinic, he was at a football game, with a heart attack. He was taken to the Cath lab; his RCA (right coronary artery) was occluded. However, in addition to the occlusion he had a right coronary artery aneurysm (dilated artery). When the balloon was dilated the artery ruptured (hole in the heart artery), and he bled to death on the way to the OR. As I tell Physicians, it is important to know what not to do. He would have been better treated with emergency coronary artery bypass. Unfortunately, some interventional cardiologists believe that if you have a blockage you need a balloon. That is the wrong answer in many circumstances. The working relationship between the cardiologist and cardiac surgeon is very important. It is important to know what not to do.

Popsicle Man

People have been seeking immortality for all of humanity. Today they can have their bodies frozen in liquid nitrogen for future reanimation from the dead. The idea is to never die and be awakened in the future. This event commonly occurs every day when an anesthesiologist or nurse anesthesia's give patients a general anesthetic awakenings them in the futures, a true miracle.

We read each winter about people, generally young, who fall through the ice in a lake or pond. They are submerged for up to 30 minutes and are rescued by friends or relatives. Transfer to the hospital, are rewarmed and survive without permanent brain or organ damage. In my prior medical practice each winter a homeless person is found outside cold with a low heart rate, low blood pressure, and a low body temperature, 31-32 degrees Celsius. They are totally unresponsive, we take them to the OR, hook them up to a heart lung machine, rewarm them to 37 degrees Celsius, When rewarmed their heart rate and blood pressure improve, they wake up and survive. Truly a miracle involving people and machines. We commonly use hypothermia (low temperatures) in patients requiring complex aortic surgery. Patients with tears in the aorta, aortic dissection, who are bleeding to death. We cool the patient to 18 degrees Celsius, turned off the Heart-Lung machine for 30 minutes and repair the tear in the aorta. The patient has no blood pressure or heart activity during the operation. Effectively they are cooled to preserve their organ function especially the brain. Once the aorta is repaired we rewarm the patient to 37 degrees Celsius. It takes 1.5-2 hours to rewarm. If all goes well the patient awakes and has normal brain function.

So we can preserve a patient with cold for a short time. When you are cold everything moves slowly and life is protected. The unlucky individual who is found cold and unresponsive is called a "bumbsickle" by some. Generally these patients have a mental illness or significant drug abuse.

Healthcare planners believe that healthcare should be uniform across the U.S... Think of the Dartmouth group. They do not understand that healthcare needs are determined by local factors. Freezing to death is a big problem in the Tetons but not in Death Valley. Heatstroke is a problem in Death Valley but not in the Tetons in the winter.

South Dakota is home to numerous Indian reservation and thousands of Indians. They have the worst healthcare in the U.S., administered by the Indian Health Service, the Federal government. One healthcare system does not provide healthcare for all. Only an idiot would believe that the Federal government is concerned about your individual health.

You Get One Chance
"The Infected Heart"

Salvage for Endocarditis

In Valvular endocarditis the valves in the heart out are destroyed by bacteria in the blood. Some of the diseases that we treat are self-inflicted. One example is intravenous (IV) drug abuse in the very young. In injecting IV drugs over time bacteria, think staph aureus, are injected into the blood. The bacteria in the blood attached to the heart valves and destroy the valve causing the valve or valves to leak. The patient develops aortic, mitral or tricuspid valve endocarditis. After 6-8 weeks of IV antibiotic to control the infection the valve is replaced with a prostatic valve. Thus, a young patient ends up with a salvage valve replacement with a new prosthetic heart valve.

The prostatic valve is made from the leaflets of a pig or cow Pericardium. This valve functions well but can be infected if the individual continues to use IV drugs. I spent some time in Everett, Washington, and in one day I saw 3 young patients (18-21 years old) with endocarditis due to IV drug use. It was very depressing one failed to respond to antibiotics and died.

A young 37-year-old female presented in shock, low blood pressure of 70mmHg systolic, at 2:00 A.M. She had been flown in by helicopter and was receiving epinephrine boluses to keep her alive. She had open-heart surgery performed three months prior for aortic valve endocarditis. She was an IV drug abuser. Her aortic valve had been eaten up by staphylococcus bacteria. Her valve was replaced and she received IV antibiotics for six weeks following the operation by a PICC line (Peripherally Inserted Central Catheter). Unfortunately she also used the PICC line for IV illicit drugs so now she had a new infection in her heart valve. Nothing could be done and she eventually died from the infection. Patients who are IV drug addicts have one shot with open-heart surgery and antibiotics to cure their heart infection. However, if they continue their addictive behavior they will die. Some diseases are self-inflicted and self-terminating.

Eaten Alive from the Inside

Rarely a patient presents to the ER with severe chest and back pain that cannot be relieved with pain medications. I asked them to describe the pain. One description that I have heard on multiple occasions is "I feel like I am being eaten alive by an animal from the inside." Generally the patient has an aortic dissection. The large vessel, aorta, above the heart has been torn and blood is dissecting between the layers of the aorta. This dissection of the blood can rupture above the heart and the patient can bleed to death. If the dissection goes up toward the brain it can cause a stroke. When that dissection goes down the descending aorta it causes the loss of blood supply to the spinal cord, this causes the severe back pain, an ascending aortic dissection, just above the aortic valve, is considered a surgical emergency. We try to repair the torn aorta with a graft to salvage the patient. We are successful 70% of the time. Survival is dependent upon the patient arriving ASAP to the ER, where the diagnosis is made. The longer the patient waits the greater the risk of death. Every minute counts. From a surgeons viewpoint this is the most difficult operation we perform and the decisions are complex. At times the repair is accomplished by cooling the patient to 18 degrees C and turning off the Heart-Lung Machine to accomplish their repair. We then rewarm them and they survive.

It's the Pump, Stupid

Technology advances have improved medical care and at the same time it has created problems, like all new technology.

In 1974-76 I worked 11-7 A.M. as an IV tech at the Baptist hospital in Memphis Tennessee. I was working on my Ph.D. in pharmacology. At that time the intravenous (IV) solutions were administered by gravity from the bag. When the IV catheter moved in the vein it affected the flow from the bag. Generally the drip rate was set to run at 125 to 150 cc/hr. it was calibrated by the drops per minute. This made the timing inaccurate, so the patient might get 500 cc in 8 hours or the intended 1000cc. This problem was solved by the invention of IV pumps. The pumps manually push a certain volume of IV fluid each minute. Thus, the accuracy of administering IV solutions was improved. This is extremely important if the patient is receiving drugs to stimulate the heart to beat, i.e. Inotropic drugs. But over time these pumps fail and have to be replaced. The company may no longer provide parts and service and the hospital has to buy new pumps. The IV pumps at the Cash Clinic were starting to fail. There were numerous meetings over years to decide upon the replacement pump. Anesthesia and the ICU nurses were in agreement on a new pump. But the pharmacy who provided the drugs wanted a Pump that could be controlled remotely by the electronic medical record, EMR. The company that provided that EMR was promoting this concept. My thoughts were that this was a bad idea; I wanted the ICU nurse at the bedside to control the infusion rate and not the computer in the pharmacy. The patient's response to multiple drugs is consistently change in there for as the heart rate and blood pressure change that nurse must change their rate of infusion, they must have minute to minute control. The pharmacy held up the decision on which IV pumps to buy. Finally one day I had a patient being transferred from the ICU to the OR for a pacemaker on drugs to support the blood pressure. The pump failed in the elevator, the patient's blood pressure dropped and the patient was in a cardiac shock entering the OR. An epinephrine Bolus was given and a different IV pump obtained. The decreased blood pressure for 10 minutes led to worsening renal failure. The patient had to have renal dialysis and eventually died.

I was upset and started to discuss the complication with the family. However, the administration at the Cash Clinic told me that we did not have to inform the family about the failure of mechanical devices. I wrote a memo about the incident because the discussion about that need for pump replacement had been ongoing for over two years. It is sad that it takes a death to encourage the corporation to make a decision. I have always tried to focus on patient care and let the chips fall where they may. Everything at the Cash Clinic was designed to suppress litigation any settlements were suppressed, the corporation does not want the customers to become aware of bad outcomes.

Harmonica Man

I first met Mr. S. in July; he had been admitted to the hospital with congestive heart failure. The heart cannot pump normal amounts of blood, fluid had built up and in his lungs and he could not breathe well. The cardiologist evaluated him; he had a leaky aortic valve, aortic regurgitation, and irregular atrial rhythm, atrial fibrillation. The leaky aortic valve is a problem, if the heart pumped out 200 ml of blood, 100 cc would leak back into the heart. The normal aortic valve does not leak. Over time, every hour your heart beats 4-5,000 times, the blood causes the heart to dilate. With dilation this size may double. As the heart increases in size, then normal size heart ejects 60-65% of the blood every beat, the ejection fraction, as the heart dilates and the ejection fraction is reduced to 30-35%. Thus, blood backs up into the lungs. The heart fails and the lungs become congested, i.e. congestive heart failure. I recommended that he have aortic valve replaced and have an ablation, to get his heart back into a normal rhythm. He said he would think about the proposed aortic valve replacement (AVR). In October he returned to clinic to see my partner, his teeth were bad, and he was scheduled for tooth extraction. Finally in December he presented for AVR and ablation. The operation went well. After the operation his daughter brought him a harmonica. Which he played for me and the staff. He enjoyed music and played in a local band. I remember patients on the basis of their interests, jobs, hobbies and family. He and his daughter were a delight. He was scheduled to be discharged on the first day of the New Year on post-operative day five follow AVR. Early that morning at 0615 eceived a call, he had gone into ventricular tachycardia, ventricular of 150bpm, and arrested. CPR was successful and he was transferred the ICU. I met him there intubated on a ventilator. He then developed ventricular fibrillation. We did CPR and pushed drugs for 30 minutes, it was not successful. He was pronounced dead at 0830 A.M. Quite a depressing day for me, I thought he was going home and now he was dead. We had placed a new valve but his heart muscle was still bad. But I believe he was going home. Yet other people that I believe will die survive. We do our best but sometimes things occur that we have no control over. This New Year's Day I will never forget the music of the Harmonica Man. Memories of life and death struggles linger for a lifetime. If I had operated sooner rather than waiting six months, would he have survived?

The Typical Patient

This would be the typical discharge summary of a patient having emergency salvage CABG.

DISCHARGE SUMMARY

Liz Coffee

Admitted: 08/03/2007
Discharged: 08/23/2007

HISTORY OF PRESENT ILLNESS: The patient is a 54-year-old female patient transferred from Sarah Brush Hospital status post myocardial infarction with cardiogenic shock. The patient did require defibrillation and intubation prior to arrival at the hospital and an intraaortic balloon pump was initiated on arrival to this facility. Cardiac Catheterization showed an occluded right, stented LAD with poor flow, high-grade as well as circumflex and diagonal stenosis. After discussion with the family, an emergency salvage coronary artery bypass graft was performed.

PAST MEDICAL HISTORY:

- Hypertension.
- Hyperlipidemia.

- GERD.
- Sleep apnea.
- History of breast cancer.
- History of uterine cancer, status post hysterectomy.
- History of small tongue mass status post removal (benign).
- History of mediastinal lymphadenopathy (benign).
- Depression.
- Degenerative joint disease.
- Uvuloplasty for sleep apnea.
- Chronic back pain.
- Morbid obesity.
- Osteopenia.
- Status post partial left breast mastectomy.
- Status post cholecystectomy.
- Status post dilatation and curettage.

- ALLERGIES
- PENICILLIN.
- ERYTHROMYCIN.
- TETANUS.

HOSPITAL PROCEDURES
1. August 05, 2007, coronary artery bypass grafting X3 with reverse saphenous vein to LAD, reverse saphenous vein to the first diagonal, reverse saphenous vein to obtuse Marginal two with ligation of left atrial appendage.
2. August 06, 2007, mediastinal closure.
3. August 20, 2007, aborted placement of implantable cardiac defibrillator.

INPATIENTS CONSULTS:
1. Diabetic Care Team
2. Wound Care Team
3. Cardiology

HOSPITAL COURSE AND COMPLICATIONS: Following the coronary artery bypass graft on August 05, 2007, the patient was taken from the operating room to the Cardiovascular Intensive Care Unit. The sternum was initially left open to closure secondary the cardiogenic shock and myocardial edema. The patient was returned to the operating room on August 06, 2007 for the sternal closure after and improvement hemodynamically. The patient received one unit of packed red blood cells on the initial CABG surgery, did not require any pacing and was on an Epinephrine and Dobutamine drip. She also remained on the intraaortic balloon pump. The intra-aortic balloon pump was discontinued on postoperative day #2 and patient was extubated on postoperative day #4, Dobutamine was also weaned off and Swan-Ganz was discontinued. The patient was able to open her eyes to commands as well as perform simple tasks. However, she did have some difficulty with her speech related to prolonged intubation. The patient was monitored for swallowing difficulties and diet was advanced from ice chips to full liquids with thickened liquids and was tolerated well. She was hemodynamically stable and had a very slow, however steady post operative recovery. She was taken to the operating room on August 20, 2007, for implantable cardiac defibrillator related to an ejection fraction of 30%. However, due to her morbid obesity, vascular access could not be obtained and the procedure was aborted. Plan will be to reschedule for AICD implantation when the patient is able to tolerate a general anesthetic.

Ms. Coffee did continue to improve hemodynamically and arrangements were made for her to be transferred to the Inpatient Rehabilitation Unit for continued PT, OT and speech therapy related to her altered ability to swallow. On postoperative day #19, the patient was hemodynamically stable and ready for discharge to the inpatient rehabilitation unit. At the time of her transfer, her temperature was 99.1, heart rate 84, respirations 18, blood pressure 108/127 systolic. She was 97% on room air. Her sternum was clean, dry, and sternum was intact as well. Graft incisions were intact with serosanguinous drainage and 2+ pitting edema bilateral lower extremities. This will continue to be followed by the wound care team and by the inpatient rehab staff.

DISCHARGE MEDICATIONS:
1. Aspirin 81 mg p.o. daily.
2. Lipitor 20 mg p.o. daily.
3. Celexa 20 mg p.o. daily.
4. Colace 100 mg p.o. b.i.d. p.r.n.
5. Pepcid 20 mg p.o. b.i.d.
6. Vicodin 5/500 mg one to two every four to six hours p.r.n. pain.
7. Novolog FlexPen 17-14-15-0.
8. Lantus 18 units subq at bedtime.
9. Lopressor 50mg p.o. b.i.d.
10. Dakin's half strength solution to the graft incisions bilateral lower extremities.

DISPOSITION AND FOLLOW-UP: The patient was discharged to the In-patient Rehabilitation Unit for physical therapy, occupational therapy, speech therapy for swallow related issues to maximize functional outcome. The patient will be schedule for follow-up visit with Dr. Cook two to three weeks following discharge from the Inpatient Rehab Unit. She will also be scheduled to follow up with Cardiology at that time.

It takes a long time to recover from a near-death experience.

Constructive Paranoia

Cardiac Surgeons can be difficult to deal with from the administrative view-point. We operate each day on patients that have a 1-3% chance of death. Thus, we deal with low-risk events, such as infections, stroke or death, but are frequent daily hazards.

The description of this paranoia was described by Jared Diamond in his book *The World until Yesterday*. He described New Guinea tribesmen, who camp out in the woods 80-90 nights per year. He did not understand their reluctance to camp adjacent to dead trees, and he did not understand their paranoia. However, upon interviewing the tribesman all had a friend or relative who had been killed by a falling tree, a low-risk event. But they were exposed to this risk on a daily basis.

Cardiac Surgeons have a similar paranoia, a low-risk of infection 1%, stroke 2% or death 2-3% for the routine elective CABG. We see this risk daily. However, if we operate on 200 patients per years then we see the complications on a weekly basis.

We know the infection rate is increased by the number of staff in the room. But, administration is always trying to expose and train new staff. Administrators want students in the room. All of this increases the infection risk, which we do not want.

New surgical techs slow us down and the chest it open longer, so the infection risk is increased. More time on the Heart-Lung Machine increases the stroke and death rate. We feel responsible when things go bad. But consultants have told all that bad results are due to systems issues. Yes, the consultants from the Space Program believe in systems complications. Whereas we look at obesity, diabetes, use of left internal mammary artery, COPD and cautery use to describe infection risk. The systems look at when pre-operative antibiotics were given and for how long. They look at the postoperative blood sugar. We look at the preoperative Hemoglobin A1C in diabetics.

To me quality is doing a perfect operation in the minimal time. The systems do not look at time because they are paid by the hour, the longer patients are in the operating room the more money they make. Additionally, the administrators at the Cash Clinic are paid to go to meetings. We understand experienced RN's and OR techs are better, they make fewer mistakes. To Administrators an RN is an RN there is no difference. Remember the primary concern at the Cash Clinic is the money. If you follow the money you understand how decisions are made.

Legend

Every profession has legends about events that have occurred to members of that profession. In my case a cardiac and thoracic surgeon.

A young, 21-year-old female was brought to the Emergency Room (ER) by ambulance. She had been involved in a motor vehicle accident (MVR) hit by another car, T bone. She had suffered blunt trauma to the left chest. We separate trauma into penetrating, gunshot wounds and stabbing and blunt crush injuries. In the ER she had a dying heart rate, 30 bpm, and no blood pressure. She was pronounced dead by the ER Physician, after CPR and fluids failed.

Her father, a thoracic surgeon arrived and performed a left Thoracotomy, an incision between the ribs. He placed a vascular clamp on the aorta to stop the bleeding and performed open cardiac massage. Her heart responded and she developed a blood pressure. The bleeding from the aorta stopped. He took her to the OR, repaired the torn aorta and she survived.

As cardiac and thoracic surgeons we try when others do not. Once we start we do not give up easily. Today the tendency is to stop; persistence produces little gain and is discouraged at many hospitals. One has to believe that success will come and be willing to accept failure in dying patients. That was the philosophy of the older surgeons who pioneered heart surgery.

Pain

Open heart surgery generally involved a sternotomy, crack the chest, as my patients say, to access the heart for an operation such as a coronary artery bypass or aortic valve replacement.

The thoughts are that this is a painful operation. If you are 80 you have little pain and then go home on Tylenol. Older patients have little pain with open-heart surgery. This is in direct contrast to my young patients, 40-50 years of age. They have major pain and are discharged home on narcotics. Thus, pain after major operation is dependent on numerous factors and one of the primary factors is age.

I tell my young patients I want you to be comfortable but I do not completely control your pain. My view is simple pain has never killed anyone; narcotics such as Vicodin have killed thousands. One other point to remember pain cannot be seen or measured. How can you adequately treat something that only someone else, the patient, can only describe?

The pain problem management started in 2001 when the joint commission on accreditation of healthcare organizations established pain management guidelines because of an imagined problem of under treating pain. As usual that media was at the forefront, if your doctor doesn't control your pain he or she is a bad doctor. Thus the prescription drug abuse problems started.

Then, the affordable Health Care Act required hospitals to do happy surveys. Of course the affordable Health Care Act made healthcare more unaffordable. The happy surveys asked are you happy with your doctor, did he or she control your pain? Are you happy with your care? Of course you are not happy because healthcare is unaffordable.

Now we see our problems with prescription drug addiction. This problem was created by bureaucratic medicine, drug companies, and patients desiring relief from the pain of life. Pain is a normal part of our survival following trauma, it guides your recovery. To suppress our perception of it is dangerous to all. Chronic pain is a different disease.

I Am Going To Stamp Out Some Disease

This is what a surgeon friend said on his way to the operating room. Stamp out is a verb meaning put an end to. Synonyms include abolish, eliminate, eradicate, exterminate, wipe out, blot out, destroy, or end. We are Physicians, and other providers, who deal with two types of disease.

Surgeons deal with anatomical diseases. There is something wrong with a body organ or body part. The appendix is ruptured and needs to be removed. The gallbladder has developed stones and needs to be removed, the hip joint has worn out, degenerated, over 80 years of use and needs to be replaced, i.e. a total hip replacement, the heart artery, i.e. coronary artery, had developed a blockage and needs to be stented or bypassed, surgeons remove, replace or repair critical body parts or organs.

When a body part fails the patient wants an attempt to improve the problem. Back problems are a common health issue. When you cannot walk due to pain, you want a repair of the problem. But things get more complicated. Sometimes the patient is told you have another more critical problem. You have a blocked heart valve, i.e. aortic stenosis that needs to be replaced of repaired before the back surgery. This is very frustrating for the patient. All they want is to be able to walk, now they have to have another procedure before the back operation. The heart problem can kill you quickly, the back problem can't kill you but can make your life miserable. We call these chronic.

There is another group of diseases, diabetes, hypertension, and elevated lipids that kill you slowly over many years. These diseases are treated with drugs, by family practice, internal medicine Physicians and other practitioners. These are chronic diseases, we cannot cure them but we can decrease their complications in treating these diseases patients live better longer. We can decrease the effects of heart artery blockages but these disease are silent. The patient wonders, do I really need these drugs? I feel great. Therefore, the tendency is to deny that one has the disease and stop the drugs. One chronic disease, obesity or fat overload, also causes anatomic problems. You can't move because you are so fat.

When President Franklin Delano Roosevelt died in 1945 at age 63 he had high blood pressure and heart failure. He died from a stroke. Reducing one's blood pressure reduces the risk of stroke, kidney failure and heart failure. In 1945 there were no medications available to treat high blood pressure, i.e. hypertension. The treatment of chronic medical problems such as high blood pressure or diabetes did not exist. Today the average U.S. citizen has access to drugs that the president did not have in 1945. The problem is getting the patient to take the drugs. After all, the diseases are silent until the stroke or heart attack occurs. The drugs cost $4.00 a month at Wal-Mart.

When you see the Physicians who treat these diseases they are interested in your age, weight, chronic level of activity, heart rate and blood pressure. They order your blood, work to monitor your blood level of hemoglobin, blood sugar, lipids and renal function. These are some of your body's essential metabolic functions. These factors help or hinder your long term survival. When your doctor tells you that you have elevated blood pressure, blood sugar, and lipids, you should exercise, lose weight and take your drugs. Hippocrates said, "Let food be the medicine and medicine your food." You need a Primary Care Physician to help you with these chronic health issues. In general these problems cannot be completely cured. There are health practices that treat illness with natural medicine, in general modern drugs work much better than herbal remedies. But many modern drugs were developed from plants and are herbal in origin.

You must keep this healthcare issue in perspective. If you walk or drive out in front of a semi truck you will die. Trauma is the leading cause of death in humans under the age of 40. Chronic diseases kill the older population.

Patient Care
The Admission

It happens thousands of times every day across the USA a 65-year-old male develops chest pain and his wife forces him to go to the emergency room. He is obese and a prior smoker.

Additionally his blood pressure had been higher than normal, around 150 mmHg systolic and his cholesterol had been elevated. He went to a doctor two years ago but refused medications for hypertension, elevated BP, and elevated cholesterol, hyperlipidemia. As we age is a normal for our blood pressure and lipids to increase. Additionally, his dad died from a heart attack at age 62.

The ER doctor evaluates him with an electrocardiogram, EKG, and blood enzymes, troponin. Both are elevated, he is having a heart attack, myocardial infarction. One of the arteries that provides blood to the heart, there are three main coronary arteries, has occluded. The ER Physician consults the interventional cardiologist on call. This cardiologist will urgently perform a cardiac catheterization. A tube will be inserted into the coronary arteries and dye will be injected to visualize the inner lining of the arteries to look for blockages or occlusions. If the EKG shows inferiors damage and a major blockage exists in the inferior coronary artery. The blockage will be cracked with a balloon and a stent will be inserted to prevent the artery from re-occluding. The object is to keep the blocked or occluded artery open to provide blood to the heart muscle. If the cardiologist is successful the heart muscle damage will be reduced.

If the artery cannot be opened of the blockage is severe, left main blockage, the patient may have emergency coronary artery bypass grafting, CABG. Ultimately the treatment is determined by the number of blockages in the coronary arteries and the number of arteries that are blocked. Generally patients that have blockages in one or two arteries receive treatment with coronary stenting. Generally it all three arteries are blocked coronary artery bypass in the best long-term fix. This patient will need to take medications, drugs, for the rest of his life. The drugs will help control the high blood pressure and cholesterol. This will help him live longer.

The Treatment

This is a complex issue because of the business of medicine. The interventional cardiologist is the first to aid the patient with the coronary stents to abort the heart attack. He or she will give the patient their future plan. In reality the best thing for the patient is to lose weight exercise and take the medications for elevated blood pressure and cholesterol.

The stenting is a quick fix for the patient they are happy and can go home in two days on medications to prevent the stent from clotting off and a new heart attack from occurring.

But the cardiac catheterization revealed blockages in the two remaining arteries providing blood flow to the heart muscle. The question now is what to do in the future. The cardiologist recommends additional stenting of the other arteries in the future. The heart surgeon never meets the patient because it is better for business, both the cardiologist and the hospital to perform multiple stents. In some hospitals, the Mother clinic in Minnesota, both a surgeon and a cardiologist will discuss treatment options with the patient. It is discussed with the patient about the need to improve his health status.

We know that patients with severe blockages in all three arteries survive longer with Coronary Artery bypass, especially diabetics. Certainly the recovery is longer after bypass surgery but survival is improved.

I have met patients with 8 to 10 coronary stents and their artery cannot be bypassed due to the stents. But the cash for the stents was a great incentive for the interventional cardiologist.

In many instances the surgeon sees the patient only after the stents have failed. Some cardiologists are ethical and involve the surgeon early in the treatment. But certainly at the Cash Clinic the primary concern is the cash and not the patient.

If an experienced surgeon is forced out and a young inexperienced surgeon is hired, then the number of stents is increased. Patients can no longer solicit the experienced surgeon and they are afraid of the young surgeon. One's reputation is determined by surgical outcomes. But the Cash Clinic does not advertise its Physicians. They come and go. Only the cash is important.

A Good Approach

A 79-year-old male develops chest pain in the afternoon, approximately 5:00 P.M. His wife convinced him to go to the VA ER. Evaluation at the VA revealed elevated ST segments in his EKG; we call this a STEMI, a type of heart attack. The other type is a non-STEMI, a heart attack without ST segment elevation. Additionally his cardiac enzymes were elevated, troponin. Most VA's do not have cardiac catheterization laboratories, so he was transferred to a private hospital. He finally made it to the catheterization lab at 11:00 P.M. at night.

The interventional cardiologist placed a catheter into the coronary arteries and injected dye. No dye went into the artery on the front of the heart. The left anterior descending artery, the most important artery in the heart was occluded. Additionally the patient had blockage in the left main artery, 70% blockage. The interventional cardiologist opened that LAD with a balloon and placed a stent. If he had not been successful in opening the artery emergency salvage bypass surgery would have been necessary. Blood thinners were started and an intra-aortic balloon pump, IABP, in the femoral artery. The heart attack was aborted when the artery was opened, the patient had coronary artery bypass, CABG scheduled in two days. He did well after the operation and returned home. The team approach to treat his lethal problem.

The Follow-up

In the Cash Clinic the interventional cardiologists make their living with stents. After the stents are done the patient is assigned to a general cardiologist who directs the medical care that is so critical for long-term outcomes. The general cardiologists make their living with medications cardiac stress tests and echocardiograms. They monitor the patient's cardiac problems over the long term. Additionally if the patient has coronary artery blockages they will care for them for years.

Coronary artery blockages which produce heart attacks are the number one killer in America. We all need to take better care of ourselves.

Medical Miracles

One of the advantages of being old, 68 years old, is that you have a historic perspective of events. I have been treating patients with heart attacks for over 30 years. I visited Russia in 1982, in patients with a heart attack, clot in coronary artery; they were passing a wire through the clot to bust it up to abort the heart attack. In America nothing was done. If a patient came in with a heart attack, we waited 2 to 3 days for recovery of the heart muscle and performed a heart catheterization, dye into coronary arteries, to identify blockages in the artery. If significant blockages existed the patient had coronary artery bypass grafting. There were no balloons to crack the blockage, i.e., PTCA, Percutaneous Coronary Angioplasty. This started in 1983-1984. There were no coronary artery stents, to keep the blockage open. These arrived in 1995. In the early years 1975 to 1995 the primary treatment for coronary artery blockages was CABG. Around 2005 interventional cardiologists started opening the coronary artery blockages in patients having a heart attack i.e. damage to the heart muscle. The standard of care today is to have the patient in the Cath lab within 90 minutes of arrival to the ER. This process created a modern miracle, if you live close to a hospital with a cardiac cath laboratory. There are approximately 1000 hospitals in the United States that perform open-heart surgery. Needless to say there are four in the state of Idaho and fifty in the city of Chicago. All of this means healthcare is better in an urban area versus a rural area. As I tell people you may have insurance but that does not mean you will get healthcare in an emergency.

Mobile Clot (Deep Vein Thrombosis and Pulmonary Embolus)

One of my most recent Emergency Salvage™ patients had this problem. Anyone who has been admitted to the hospital of had a major operation has received shots IN their abdomen, i.e. Heparin and compression boots on their legs. This is all aimed to prevent deep vein thrombosis. When we have been traumatized by an operation, abdominal operation, or an accident we are immobile. Thus, we do not ambulate and our activity level is diminished. A patient having a major operation such as a hip replacement may be immobile on the OR table for 3 to 4 hours. Additionally we may not walk for 2 to 3 days. The combination of trauma, you were stabbed, and inability to walk may lead to clots forming in your leg veins. When we are cut our body form clots to stop the bleeding. When the clots occur in the leg veins, we call this deep vein thrombosis. If the clots break off when you ambulate they float to the lungs and lodge there. We call this a pulmonary Embolus. If a clot is large it may obstruct blood flow through the lungs and result in low blood pressure and cardiac arrest. Generally the clots are small the lung catches them and breaks them up and no harm occurs. Generally the patient is treated with blood thinners for three months.

The patient that I care for was three days out from an abdominal operation to remove her uterus following the delivery of her child. She was 35 years old, feeling well, up walking, ready for discharge from the hospital when her heart rate increased to 130 beats per minute and her blood pressure could not be obtained. Closed cardiac and pulmonary resuscitation (CPR) was started. A tube was placed in her trachea. She did not respond to the drugs to elevate her blood pressure. I arrived 15 minutes after the arrest; her pupils were fixed and dilated. Think brain death. The decision was made by me to place her on a machine to support her heart and lungs. I thought that she had suffered a large pulmonary Embolus and blood could not move through the lungs. This happened on a Saturday morning, an OR team was in house, they brought the instruments and the supplies to open her right groin. The perfusionist arrived with the ECMO machine, extra corporal membrane oxygenator, within 20 minutes. The cannulas were placed in the artery and veins and the patient placed on the ECMO. The total CPR time was one hour. The big question was will she be brain dead, did her brain receiving an adequate blood flow during the hour of CPR. A miracle occurred, due to a large number of well-trained medical people she woke up that night. She was on the ECMO machine for four days and a ventilator for an additional two days. She was saved by people and machines. Of note she had been on blood thinners after the operation and they had failed.

This was an emergency salvage treatment for massive pulmonary Embolus. Additionally, as I pointed out no informed consent was obtained from either the patient of the family. There was no time for legal concerns. I discussed this with the husband and parents after the arrest and they agreed it was necessary. This story had a happy ending, she survived. However, if she had died, some administrator or lawyer would have complained about the unnecessary attempt to save her life. After all she was dead, no blood pressure and fixed the dilated pupils of the eye. Remember critics are people who come in after the battle and shoot the wounded. The world is full of journalists who are critics. They are the true "death panels" in our society.

The Murmur

Many patients are confused about heart murmurs. They have been told that they have a heart murmur and believe that is a bad thing. I see the elderly, 80-year-old patients for Valvular heart disease, generally aortic stenosis. They have an abnormal murmur of aortic valve (blockage). A comment they often make is: I have had a murmur since childhood. What has changed?

I say, everyone who is alive has a murmur. When we listen to your heart with our stethoscope we listen to the valves open and close, the movement of blood through the heart produces a normal murmur. If there is no sound, your heart is not pumping, and you are dead.

Then I say you have an abnormal murmur of a blocked heart valve. The sound of your heart has changed, this valve is calcified, blocked and blood going through the valve produces a harsh sound every time it beats. We are pretty good at the diagnosis of aortic stenosis (blocked) and mitral regurgitation (leaky) valves. However, whenever a Physician (or health care provider, if you work at the Cash Clinic) hears an abnormal murmur you get an echocardiogram. It's good to have a normal murmur.

Old Blood

This was an interesting day that highlighted the complexity of open-heart surgery. The OR techs set up the sterile field, supplies and instruments, for over an hour before the patient comes into the room to receive anesthesia.

This morning as the techs were placing instruments out in sequence to be used they noticed the aortic cross clamp was encrusted with old blood. It had not been washed adequately in Central supply. Central supply cleans and sterilizes the open heart instruments. The old blood contaminated the sterile field, at least by U.S. standards. The field was torn down and a different set of instruments and supplies were obtained. Thousands of dollars of sponges and supplies were discarded. The patient was late coming into the OR by one hour. Every one anesthesia, perfusion and surgeons lost hours of time. All of this was done to decrease the risk of an infection following the insertion of a new aortic valve and coronary artery bypass. The patient was an obese, 260 lb. diabetic. It takes a good OR crew and a lot of time, effort and money to provide good OR care. In this case they were outstanding.

The People I Never Meet

During the latter part of my career, I worked in the UP, Upper Peninsula of Michigan. A Geo graphically isolated part of the U.S. Marquette has the only cardiac surgery program in the UP. Patients drive from great distances, 3 hours by car, for emergency cardiac care. I was on call two weeks at a time so I heard about many patients who did not make it to our emergency room alive.

One of my first calls was from Copper Harbor. An 82-year-old male presented to their ER with abdominal pain for eight hours. A CT scan revealed an abdominal aortic aneurysm, AAA. The patient received at fluids and blood. But in the case of a ruptured AAA blood is leaking from the abdominal aorta out into the abdomen. The patient bleeds to death over a few hours. The UP Marquette sent their helicopter 45 minutes to Copper Harbor, but the patient bled to death before the helicopter arrived. His only hope was to have gone to the ER sooner. Where I practiced in east central Illinois there were 4 hospitals that could care for this problem within 1 hour by car. Medical care is more difficult to obtain in an isolated rural area. Unfortunately many confuse healthcare with health insurance. Just because you have insurance does not make medical care available.

Later in the week another call came from an ER 30 minutes away by car. A 75 year old man had developed severe chest pain at 0900 A.M. he presented to the ER at 1400 and was diagnosed with an ascending aortic dissection, blood was leaking into his aorta and he was bleeding to death. The aorta is the large blood vessel moving blood around the body. His heart rate was low, 60bpm, and his blood pressure was low 80mmHg, normal 120mmHg. He received appropriate care IV fluids and blood. I drove to our ER to meet them in transfer for emergency salvage surgery. He suffered a cardiac arrest during transport and CPR was not successful. He was pronounced dead by an ER Physician. I never met him, but I did see his CT scan and I read his obituary in the paper.

I still have nightmares about the patients I have never met and the ones that I did meet for emergency surgery. I have been involved with hundreds of these patients. All of them nightmares, but they have to be balanced by the patients who survived their near-death experience.

When I would get a critical letter from the Cash Clinic administrators, I would pull out a letter from a grateful patient, I have hundreds. The good thoughts help to suppress the bad experience of working at a multi-specialty clinic where the primary focus is the cash.

Anyone Can Do It

This is the thought of modern corporate medicine. Modern heart and lung surgery requires the expertise of many Physicians. My patients require excellent anesthesia. The patient must remain stable during anesthesia for the operation. They must remain still, no movement, have control of pain and remained hemodynamically stable, the heart rate and blood pressure is normal. In patients with bad hearts and lungs this processes is difficult. The medical team that provides this are MD anesthesiologist and RN nurse anesthesia. At the Cash Clinic the anesthesia care model was one MD overseeing three RN nurse anesthesia. But that is incorrect. The MD Anesthesiology trained can have an additional year training in cardiac anesthesia. We had three Physicians that had the additional years training. I wanted them to be responsible for heart and lung operation. The administrative head of anesthesiology said NO. We spent three months in conflict and finally she agreed a separate cardiac call schedule with seven nurse anesthesia RN's, but she would not agree to this for pulmonary or lung cases. She wanted no specified staff for these cases. Anyone can do these cases.

This remained a long-term base of contention. In a certain sense, lung cases were more difficult from a technical viewpoint. These patients required a special endotracheal tube, a double lumen tube. The double lumen tube allows the lung to be collapsed so we as surgeons can remove a portion of the lung, to remove lung cancer. Over the years there was considerable difficulty in placing these tubes by both MD and RN anesthesia. The philosophy remained anyone can do it. As I remarked, yes anyone can do it, especially when there is little concern about doing it correctly. As I was getting ready to leave the Cash Clinic that bad complication occurred an inexperienced nurse tore a hole in the right lungs bronchus. The patient nearly died with this complication. The patient arrested twice during the repair but survived. In my view this was malpractice, but the patient never really understood what happened.

After I left the Cash Clinic I spent time in Washington State with all M.D. anesthesias who only did heart and lung surgery. They did it every day and were excellent. A great experience for me and the patients.

As surgeons we spend a lot of time creating the medical care that is best for the patient. Sometimes our biggest obstacle is the hospital administration. Corporations are focused on the cash especially at the Cash Clinic.

Medical specialists exist because our patients have different and unique healthcare needs.

Follow the Money

The Cash Clinic is one of the 10 most profitable hospitals in the United States. The 2013 profit came in at $163.5 million or $2,080 per patient. See *News Gazette* May 2016. But the Cash Clinic is a not for profit hospital, a true misnomer. Thus the Cash Clinic is great in harvesting money from their patients.

In America 8% of healthcare dollars go to administrators at the hospital, versus 3% in the rest of the world. The Cash Clinic has hundreds of administrators with MBA's whose job is to separate you from your money using the healthcare system. The administrators make millions off of our patients.

From the Physician's viewpoint, of the money that was billed for my services for cardiac surgery 60% went to the clinic. I kept 40% of collected money. The Cash Clinic recruits young Physicians directly out of training and offers them a good salary. Generally after a few years they leave for better opportunities. That Cash Clinic keeps these Physicians out of town by using a restrictive covenant. In Illinois it is legal to restrict Physicians local practice but not lawyers, thus the Cash Clinic keeps out any local competition, great for the corporation but bad for the patients and their money. This is corporate medicine at its best, harvest the money. The goal is to create a local monopoly.

The cash would not pay their neurosurgeons well so they left plenty of money for administrators but not physicians or nurses.

The EMR
(Electronic Medical Record)

The unaffordable Health Care Act spent billions of dollars on the EMR. Because of this you spent little time with your Physician or nurse. Their job was to enter data on you, they became a data entry technician. The typical house staff spent 40% of their time in front of the computer and 12% of their time with the patient. The computer is cold, insufficient and lacking of emotion. For the Cash Clinic the EMR improved billing so the money flow increased. Everyone gained in money flow except the patient and the Physician.

The patient paid for the EMR by increased taxed and cost of Health Care. Nearly $30 billion dollars of government stimulus over ten years. The Physician paid with decreased income, one sees 20% fewer patients using the EMR, your time is eaten up by the computer.

The Cash Clinic uses Epic systems, based in Verona, Wisconsin, for their EMR. Epic controls half of the marketplace for EMR. It is your medical data that Epic has, but try to get your medical records from the Cash Clinic or Epic. Epics proposed pricing to share records with other insurers is four cents per message sent. In the past you could get your medical records from your Physician. Today at the Cash Clinic all Physicians are employee and they own your data that you paid for. The corporation, Cash Clinic believes that they own you and your data. Many Physicians were fired from the Cash Clinic for failure to embrace the EMR. One of our best internal medicine Physicians was terminated; he moved his practice to Indianapolis to get outside the restrictive covenant that prevented him from practicing locally. The hospital notes became longer with cut and paste, no one had the time to read them, but billing increased. The Cash Clinic benefited greatly more control and threats. Small group Physicians retired early. Small Group practices bankrupted by upfront expense of locked into ineffective systems. Hours consumed by difficult data entry unrelated to patient care. Only the hospitals received the $35,000 per Physician for training. The training programs were poor and the time requirements, three days, to train were worthless.

Medicine was treated by the politicians as industry such as a modern manufacturing plant. The purpose of the EMR as envisioned by the Obama Administration in 2008 was to provide a transition from volume based to value based payments. A simple explanation, the government wanted to change how Physicians were paid and shift payments to the hospital. They would no longer pay me for performing coronary artery bypass on a patient; they would pay the hospital who would determine my fee. There are few thoracic surgeons being trained. One reason is the duration of training 7 to 9 years after medical school. Another is you do not know how or what your salary will be. The Cash Clinic will determine that figure.

If you want to know more about the chaos of the EMR, read *Transitional Chaos or Enduring Harm? The EHR and the Disruption of Medicine* by Lisa Rosenblum M.D. This system, EMR, totally disrupted the Physician and patient relationships. Big government at work.

Bad Things Clump Together

In my line of work I see life-threatening problems that affect my patients, friends, and family in a bad way. Eventually a bad event or human defect occurs in all of us.

I work with patients with two lethal problems acute cardiac problems and lung cancer. Heart attacks are the leading cause of death in the U.S., with 600,000 people dying annually of heart disease. In patients diagnosed with lung cancer, 70% are dead within a year. Smoking contributes to both of these lethal problems. I have had patients with successful treatment of their heart disease die of lung cancer. Additionally I have successful treated lung cancer, with lung removal, and have the patient eventually die of heart disease. Even if you survive successful treatment, the combination of a bad heart and lungs leads to a miserable existence for the remainder of your life.

As a surgeon things are either too busy or too slow in our practice, because we see patients with end of life problems. They present to the ER or to the EMT's by a 911 call.

Bad things clump together. We see no aortic dissections for months, and then we treat three patients in a week. We see no Cath lab disasters for months and then we see three in two weeks. Bad things clump together in threes for us and our patients. I remember a patient who had a heart attack treated with a stent. A week later a second heart attack treated with successful coronary artery bypass. Then six weeks later he was killed in a motor vehicle accident. When a bad event occurs or a near miss and you survive, pay close attention in the near term to avoid a second bad even. Bad events in life are clumped together in groups of three. When life is going bad it is good to be paranoid. We as thoracic surgeons practice constructive paranoia. It is good to be paranoid about low-risk events such as driving a vehicle. When events are going bad for my patients or myself I try to limit daily risks. In the OR we surround ourselves with staff that we know and do not try anything new. We want a standard routine for open-heart surgery, No deviation from the norm. How does one limit the daily risks of life? Pay attention to the small details. Avoid distractions such as TV's computers and cell phones. Don't speed in the car and control your emotions. Most importantly listen and think about prior bad events. What about the health risks of life? It is important to realize that what you do today controls your future health. Avoid the extremes of daily life. Too much sun on your skin in your youth produces skins cancer. No sunglasses future cataracts, too much food and drink produces obesity and diabetes. Remember your health is dependent on you and you only. Eat and drink in moderation. Exercise daily and check your weight monthly. Check your blood pressure and heart rate daily. Take a weekly walk with nature. Acquire a pet to further enjoying life. Have a friend or loved one check your skin for new spots or growing spots monthly. Realize that when you reach middle age, 40s, your body changes. Your weight, cholesterol and blood pressure increase as you age. Of most importance exercise improves all three problems. Losing weight improves both cholesterol and elevated blood pressure, hypertension. Listen to your body as it changes over the years. Your perception of your health is very important. If you are diagnosed with a medical problem educate yourself. Do not take drugs unless you know the benefits and side effects. Avoid illicit drugs and narcotics. Denial of disease is a lethal problem. We all develop diseases as we age. Try to understand yours; we all develop gray hair and wrinkles. Develop hobbies, it's important to realize the graveyard is full of irreplaceable people. I remember my patients by their life stories.

A Successful Operation but a Bad Outcome

Medicine is both simple and complicated. Patient care is a complex art form. It is not a science because it involves humans and their behavior.

A 62-year-old female presented to the hospital with vision changes in her left eye and right sided weakness. These symptoms resolved in 30 minutes, we call this a TIA, transit ischemic attack. A small clot moved from her neck artery, carotid, to her brain. TIA's are markers for future strokes. Her left carotid artery, symptomatic side, had already been operated on, carotid endarterectomy. We remove the blockage and place a patch on the artery. However, this lady continued to smoke heavily, 1 ½ packs per day. Her carotid ultrasound, sound waves, indentified a blockage, revealed in her right carotid artery. Double trouble for this lady. What is the best treatment for this lady? Operate on the symptomatic left carotid, the high-grade right carotid or both at the same time.

The surgeon decided to operate on the symptomatic left side with the clot. My former partner would have done both sides, the aggressive approach. The redo operation was done on the left side and it was successful. The patient went to the ICU awake and alert doing well. A successful operation. The patient goes to the ICU following operation and does well until midnight. She develops left sided weakness which means her right carotid artery is now forming a clot. The Physician's Assistant, PA, working with the surgeon is called. He does nothing and does not call the surgeon about the patients change. The critical care Physician calls the interventional radiologist who places a carotid stent in the blocked artery, in the midst of the evolving stroke. The stent opens the artery but the patient has suffered a large stroke with brain swelling. The neurosurgeons remove the bone of the brain, craniotomy, to relieve the swelling of the brain. The operation is a success, all three operations were a success but the patient developed brain death and died two days later.

From a quality viewpoint how could this bad outcome, death, have been altered?

- The patient could have stopped smoking, reducing the progression of carotid blockage.
- The operation could have been done in the Right carotid artery, the highest grade blockage.
- The operation could have been performed on both carotid arteries.
- A blood thinner could have been started immediately after the left carotid endarterectomy.
- The surgeon could have been contacted directly at midnight and the ride side operated.

This incident highlights surgical decision-making and postoperative care. Both are critical for good outcomes. In this instance the Physician's Assistant failed the patient. Successful operations do not always lead to good patient outcomes.

Malpractice

This is a different issue. People develop health issues and die daily. The goal of the healthcare system is to extend and improve the patient's life. Unfortunately, this goal is not always achieved. I have been personally involved in litigation eight times over 30 years which involved operations in approximately 7000 patients. But, any Physician who accepts responsibility for a patient's medical care has been sued. In my line of work I operate on patients that already have infections, have evolving stroke and are actively dying from their heart attack. Thus, bad outcomes are predetermined. Generally the problem is not life-threatening, an infection in the leg following harvest of a vein or an IV that infiltrates causing arm swelling. I was not the Physician to insert the IV, but the complication occurred in a patient I operated on. So I was sued. The Cash Clinic paid the patients damages because their insurance covers all hospital employees.

The Cash Clinic is unique in that it's Malpractice Company that they own, is headquartered in the Cayman Islands. They self-insure their entire corporation, the Cash Corporation. Of course no corporation wants to be known for malpractice verdicts, especially in excess of one million dollars. So any settlement is suppressed. Part of the settlement agreement against the corporation involves the victim or family of victim agreeing to say nothing about the money received. This allows the Cash Clinic to keep their sterling local reputation. After all they have paid Health Grade® hundreds of thousands of dollars to advertise how good they are in providing healthcare. The advertised top 100 or top 50 or top 10 involves a payment to Health

Grades®. Thus, the Cash Clinic is marketed as providing world class care. Certainly this is true if your comparison in the world is the Congo in Africa.

So the local paper headlines that would say "Patient dies of narcotic overdose following knee surgery at the Cash Clinic" are suppressed. The patient, who died, receives nothing but the family receives a million to say nothing bad about the Cash Corporation.

In my time as head of surgery at the Cash Clinic I observed this with surgical malpractice issues. New technology such as endoscopic gallbladder removal, allows earlier discharge from the hospital. But it introduced new problems.

In the open removal of the gallbladder we identified and injected the common bile duct, it was rarely injured. In endoscopic removal of the gallbladder the common duct was more commonly injured. One young general surgeon, at the Cash Clinic, injured the common duct on multiple occasions. His operative injuries were bad, he ligated the common duct and the patient suffered irreversible injury. Unfortunately, there is a learning curve for all new technology.

Let's play a game called "Is this malpractice?" A young male with appendicitis and lymphoma goes to the OR for endoscopic appendectomy. The removal of the appendix goes well, but the surgeon sees a mass in the stomach. He attempts to remove the mass, the resection area bleeds and the patient dies in the OR. Was this malpractice? Or did the patient die from complications of appendicitis. A young female is involved in a motor vehicle accident with blunt trauma to abdomen. She is admitted to the hospital and her blood count decreases, she is bleeding in her abdomen. She is taken to the OR as an emergency for open exploration of the abdomen. The surgeon opens this area, a gush of blood rushes out, he places his hand into the area and removes her left kidney. She bleeds to death in the OR. What is in this malpractice? Or was this a complication of her motor vehicle accident.

We will never know the answer to the malpractice question. The Cash Clinic settled these cases. How much money was paid out, we don't know. But most importantly no bad local publicity courtesy of the lawyers.

However, sometimes malpractice is obvious. An inexperienced chest surgeon at the Cash Clinic leaves a sponge inside the chest in association with an operation. He sends the patient out of town to have it removed.

The outside surgeon refuses, and states this is malpractice, remove it yourself. A settlement occurs, no bad publicity. We know about this incident, the staff and Physicians at the Cash Clinic. Would they send their family and friends to this surgeon? The answer is NO. But what about the patients who are insured by the Cash Corporations' healthcare insurance? If they go outside the system they have to pay a 20% deductible. Do not get locked into a single corporation's insurance product. It may be convenient but you have no selection of medical services.

Moving On

It was a nice January day in 2015. I had made an appointment with Shane, my older son, to go out for lunch. He is a sheriff's captain in Champaign County. At his job level he was involved in the politics of law enforcement. He asked me how much longer I was going to work at the Cash Clinic; I had been there 25 years. I said I hope to work a few more years but they could fire me today. Our contract had a no cause portion. I could be fired without cause at anytime.

I discussed the changes in the Cash Clinic. Physicians were now employee and we had little input into how the organization is run. Now that we were a vertically integrated company, the Cash Foundation had bought the insurance company, Cash Care, and the focus was on the money.

Dr. Jim Lyer was now the CEO for the entire foundation. His $1.4 million dollar yearly salary was dependent upon the monetary growth of the Cash Foundation. He had recently hired a third cardiac surgeon, Dr. Gary Weedy, so our overhead costs had increased $500,000, the salary to be paid to Dr. Weedy. The question was, how do we increase our clinical service to increase the cash? The Cash Corporation is always looking ahead to replace older Physicians, especially when they would not give a retirement date.

Dr. Matt Gether was determined to start a program to implant permanent left ventricular assist devices (LVAD). Dr. Gether got his name when he came to the Cash Clinic. He was between marriages and was out to get the nurses who were available. He wanted his females young and dumb. After his second marriage failed he decided to become an administrator.

He worked his way up from interventional cardiologist, to head of cardiology, and finally to medical director for the Cash Clinic. His job was to grow the money pie. He believed he was in control of the Cash Clinic.

His decision to start a new program with a new surgeon directly out of training was a poor decision. Dr. Weedy's first six months were highlighted by poor technical skills, irregular decision-making and high morality's for cardiac surgery. But Dr. Gether and I had started a TAVR, trans-aortic valve implant program, and he believed the LVAD program would be easy. I didn't want anything to do with this program. I had been implanting temporary LVAD's for 10 years, as a bridge to recovery or transplant. The EMCO program extracorporeal membrane oxygenator made the program a possibility. But a young surgeon has no independent experience.

The other administrator for the Heart and Vascular Center was a Dr. Mocryer. Dr. Mocryer practiced at a branch of the Cash Clinic in Danville. Dr. Gether wanted Dr. Mocryer to be a director because he would do what he wanted. Many administrators want weak people dependent upon them. At the Cash Clinic Physicians do not have the opportunity to evaluate their administrators. Physicians are evaluated on a yearly basis but not the administrators. Should not the administration as a whole-in particular the decision makers, leadership personnel individually be reviewed annually by the practitioners of surgery and medicine—the actual providers of healthcare. Administration numbers are 8% of the hospitals positions. Thus, there is a lot of administration waste and obesity.

Dr. Mocryer and I did not get along; he was a poor clinician and administrator. But he doubled his salary by becoming an administrator. The other advantage was he could bury any quality issues that would arise from his care. So a bleed from a cardiac catheterization he performed in which the patient nearly died, was never discussed at quality meeting. Additionally, Dr. Mocryer was a foreign trained Physician and most of the cardiologist at the Cash Clinic are foreign. The Cash Clinic likes Physicians with green cards; they are easier to control, versus American-born Physicians. They have a harder time finding a new job if they are fired.

We had hired a new Physician's Assistant, PA, to train for the OR. The first week of his orientation, we were doing a case on a Friday afternoon, and he disappeared. He did not show up for the patient's operation. He was

Muslim and was praying at the mosque. I wrote him up. Dr. Mocryer was upset, he is a Muslim. It's sad when one uses their religion to avoid their duty to sick patients. After I left the PA was eventually fired, over other issues. His religion was more important that his job. As I was leaving the restaurant I told Shane. These people are no longer concerned about the patients, it is the money. They may fire me any day.

I returned to the clinic to see patients and received a notice to attend a meeting on the eighth floor. The floor of administrators. It was a meeting with Dr. Gether and Dr. Mocryer. The statement was "We are mad at you and you are fired with one year's salary as compensation $500,000." Over the past two years I have spent time at four different hospitals performing open-heart surgery. It has been a good experience for me. The support systems are different from hospital to hospital. Some better than the Cash Clinic and some worse. But it is obvious to me that the Cash Clinic was concern about the money more than any other hospital. Try to avoid the Cash Clinic for your care, if possible. There are a lot of better hospitals available to you. Shop around.

Who Are You?

This is the big problem, for corporate health care such as the Cash Clinic. It is difficult to monitor the 3 to 4000 employees providing healthcare. From housekeeping, who keeps the facility clean, to nurse who provide direct patient care. The solution is an employee badge that everyone must wear. There are many areas of the hospital that you cannot enter without a badge. In the large corporation no one knows the employees, so they are assigned a number. The bean counters look at you only as a number. Everyone is tracked by their badge number and log in to the computer. Employees move from job to job trying to find a comfortable area to work in. but they really do not enjoy their job. There is the never ending corporate compliance, the computer updates. Daily there are mandates from management. Running a 300-bed hospital is difficult, especially when the employees are unknown. The Physicians are tracked by states, hospitals and the Federal government. There is a small army of credentials employees who track our training and outcomes from medical school to retirement. We are recredentialed for hospital privileges, to provide care, every two years. I have a provider number from the Federal government. Each state in which I have practiced has a unique number for me. The hospitals all have a different employee number for me. Each healthcare insurer, Medicaid, Medicare, VA or private insurers Blue Cross Blue Shield, have a different number. All of this has been set up to control your healthcare.

The Federal government wants all Physicians to be employees of a large corporation. Therefore, if the corporation is controlled so are the Physicians. Individual Physicians cannot afford the costs of the Electronic Medical Record, malpractice, buildings, employees and time spent collecting money from the insurance companies. Thus, the Federal government and Cash Clinic control your healthcare. The goal of the Cash Clinic is to keep any competition from coming into town. Essential is the restrictive covenant, if a Physician leaves the Cash Clinic, they cannot practice locally for three years.

As a young child I went to our family Physician, Dr. Kinley, for my care and shots. He gave his own shots and care. He had a receptionist to run the office. We paid cash no insurance. At that time 1957 there was no open-heart surgery. Now we have an army of healthcare providing care that in many circumstances is unnecessary. Go to the ER with chest pain and you get serum enzyme levels, EKG and CT scan of the chest. You are told it is all normal your heart is fine. The cost you have no idea because your insurance covered it. So really it is free as long as you keep your job and insurance. Now the Cash Clinic knows who you are and wants you to buy their insurance product. But remember that corporations know you as a number on the computer. Their interest is your money not your health. When I go back to the Cash Clinic I am known as a number and date of birth. Even though I worked there for 25 years no one knows me. The receptionist wants to know if I have been out of the country. My answer allows them to collect additional money to treat Ebola patients. They do not know me but my presence allows them to collect cash.

Do This or You Will Die

This is something that I would rarely say to patients or families. Maybe 2-3 times per year. Generally, I performed 200 open-heart surgeries per year; I would use this expression to patients that I believed have only a few hours to live. Typically these patients have had successful CPR and need to go to OR immediately. The other groups of patients have 99% left main stenosis with low blood pressure.

One afternoon I met a patient who had emergency cardiac catheterization for chest pain, he had 99% Left main stenosis, which means 70-80% of the blood supply was at jeopardy. I told him he should have emergency coronary bypass grafting (CABG). He laughed and said a doctor had told him that 2 years ago. That doctor was not a cardiac surgeon, a son was with him, and I discussed the need for emergency CABG. He did not believe me. Cardiology admitted the patient to the Intensive Care Unit (ICU). That night I received a call from the ICU the patients' blood pressure was low and he felt that he was going to die. By the time I got to the hospital he was dead.

If a gray-headed heart surgeon tells you that you need emergency open-heart surgery, please listen. But it is you decision, not mine.

The End

In the end everyone dies, but it is important to understand that the powers that exist other than your family and church are aligned against you. The government, i.e. Medicare, believe that 40% of your healthcare in expenses occur in your last year of life. Thus, insurers want to limit their expenses if you get really sick. You and your employer paid into Medicare your whole career, but the government and other insurers believe that it is their money, not yours. Thus, they want to convince you that further medical care is futile.

The hospital, if you are really sick, has no incentive to keep you alive. They are paid a fixed amount, i.e. Diagnostic Related Group (DRG) for your specific care such as pneumonia. The longer you are alive the more money they lose. Additionally, if they convince you to go into hospice, it is a different pot of money. Therefore, they want you out of the hospital, comfortable with end-of-life care.

Physicians have no incentive to keep you alive, at the Cash Clinic they are salaried employees. The hospital doctors work 12-hour shifts for a week and then they are gone. Continuity of care doesn't really exist. If you get worse then the next doctor may encourage end-of-life care.

In my line of work, the hospital wants a 2% 30-day mortality rate for CABG. They discourage us from operating on a patient who is dying. Of course this is the patient who benefits most, 100% chance of a death versus 50% survival rate. One suggestion to you, if you are truly sick get to know your doctors and nurses.

CPSIA information can be obtained
at www.ICGtesting.com
Printed in the USA
LVHW03s2144250818
588166LV00019B/249/P